MATH

LESSONS
FOR A
LIVING
EDUCATION

level 2

Angela O'Dell
& Kyrsten Carlson

First printing: March 2016

Fifth printing: June 2019

Master Books®, P.O. Box 726, Green Forest, AR 72638

Master Books® is a division of the New Leaf Publishing Group, Inc.

ISBN: 978-0-89051-924-0
ISBN: 978-1-61458-489-6 (digital)

Unless otherwise noted, Scripture quotations are from the New King James Version of the Bible.

Printed in the United States of America

Please visit our website for other great titles: www.masterbooks.com

For information regarding author interviews, please contact the publicity department at (870) 438-5288.

Dedication

To all the little children, whom He Loves.

Master
Books®
A Division of New Leaf Publishing Group
www.masterbooks.com

Scope and Sequence

Features: The suggested weekly schedule enclosed has easy-to-manage lessons that guide the reading, worksheets, and all assessments. The pages of this course are perforated and three-hole punched so materials are easy to tear out, hand out, grade, and store. Teachers are encouraged to adjust the schedule and materials needed in order to best work within their unique educational program.

Lesson Scheduling: Students are instructed to read the pages in their book and then complete the corresponding section provided by the teacher. Assessments that may include worksheets, activities, quizzes, and tests are given at regular intervals with space to record each grade. Space is provided on the weekly schedule for assignment dates, and flexibility in scheduling is encouraged. Teachers may adapt the scheduled days per each unique student situation. As the student completes each assignment, this can be marked with an "X" in the box.

🕐	**Approximately 30 minutes per lesson, five days a week, for 36 weeks**
🔑	**Answer keys for worksheets are available online: www.masterbooks.com/classroom-aids**
📑	**Worksheets and quizzes are included throughout course**
📄	**Designed for grade 2 in a one-year course**

Course Description

Welcome to the second book in the **Math Lessons for a Living Education** series! You will find that *Math Lessons for a Living Education* is a unique approach to learning math. A blend of stories, copy work, oral narration, and hands-on experience brings the concepts to life and invites the child to explore the world around them. The tone of this math book is meant to speak personally to each child, and the method easily adapted to any teaching style.

The first 30 lessons have a story about the twins, taught through hands-on learning. Sometimes, this lesson is learned by the twins' explorations in nature. After the story, there are exercises for students to practice the lesson they learned and to review what they have learned earlier. "Quizzes" or reviews, whichever you want to use them as, are in the form of "letters to family and friends." The twins want to show them what they have been learning, and they need students to help them! Students show what they have learned by writing the letters for the twins. The last 6 lessons are focused reviews, covering topics learned throughout the first 30 lessons.

- ✔ Review addition and subtraction, and basic numbers up to 100
- ✔ Explore new concepts like word problems, skip counting money and time
- ✔ Learn how to read bar graphs and line graphs, as well as understand basic measurement
- ✔ Identify place values, regrouping concepts, and measurement with a thermometer.

Teaching mathematics as a living subject

This book is the continuing story of Charlie and Charlotte, who are learning that life is full of learning opportunities! As you read their story, students will be drawn into the adventure along with the twins. They will learn about numbers, shapes, place value, adding, and subtracting. They will also learn about the seasons, geography, and the love of family. They will be invited to join the twins on their living math adventures. I hope you have a grand time on this adventure. Have a wonderful time exploring and learning!

As a teacher and a mother, I have discovered that true education is based on relationships: the relationship the child makes with the amazing concepts in the world around them; the relationship the teacher and the child make with each other; and most importantly and ultimately, the relationship the child makes with their Creator. It is built on discovering the God of the Universe — the One who holds the universe in His hands but at the same time, lovingly indwells the heart of a little child. The story in Book 2 is meant to reach into a child's world, grab their attention and invite them into the learning process. The concepts are not taught through drill only, but also through encouraging the student to hone their critical thinking skills and think outside of the book. This curriculum teaches the student math, but it is not result-oriented, focusing only on grades; instead it is skill and process-oriented. I have discovered that it is in the everyday that we grow and become who we are meant to be. It is in the little discoveries all along the path of life that we grow, learn, develop, and discover who God is and, in turn, see ourselves the way He sees us. Math concepts are learned well, as it is learned in the context of living, in the midst of discovery, and through the worldview glasses that focus on the bigger picture.

Optional resources in back: If you feel that your student could use a little more practice, use the Larger Addition Mat or Larger Subtraction Mat from the appendix to practice the concepts being taught. These are included in the back and can be laminated or slipped into a page protector. The use of these mats is optional. If an exercise mentions using a mat, please feel free to use it according to your student's needs. They are meant to give students extra practice in the concept being taught in the lesson.

About manipulatives

In the back of the book, you will find a manipulatives section. It is imperative that you gather these before you start the book. You will need these resources:

- [ ] contact paper and construction paper
- [ ] large index cards
- [ ] brass fasteners
- [ ] crayons, markers, and colored pencils
- [ ] glue or paste
- [ ] hole punch and hole reinforcers
- [ ] rings to keep flashcards together
- [ ] a plastic shoe box with lid in which to store manipulatives
- [ ] stickers to use for flashcards (optional but helpful)
- [ ] pictures from old magazines
- [ ] poster board (several large pieces)
- [ ] dried beans, buttons, craft sticks all work well
- [ ] 4 containers for your Place Value Village (1-extra large, 1-large, 1-medium, 1-small)
- [ ] snack-size baggies
- [ ] foot ruler (with inches marked)
- [ ] simple indoor/outdoor thermometer (non-digital)
- [ ] 4 square pieces of material which measure 12 inches on all sides (4 different light colors would be best, or white/off white)

- [ ] fabric or permanent markers in bright colors
- [ ] your favorite color of yarn and a large needle with a large eye
- [ ] thread in whatever color you wish in a sewing needle
- [ ] material (whatever kind you wish) for backing (about 24 inches square)
- [ ] thin batting (about 24 inches square) optional
- [ ] fabric scissors
- [ ] measuring tape
- [ ] iron
- [ ] straight pins
- [ ] candy thermometer
- [ ] measuring devices (cup, pint, quart, gallon)

Note about money manipulatives: you will need to have the following money available for students to use throughout this book:

- 10 dimes
- 20 nickels
- 100 pennies
- 4 quarters
- 5 $1 bills

Right Brain Flash Cards

I include these special flash cards in this math curriculum because I have found through almost two decades of teaching math that every student connects better when asked to use both sides of their brain to engage in a new concept. Memory is enhanced. Recall is improved. And personalization of the learning process is brought to a much higher level than simple rote memory facilitates. In short, when we engage both sides of our brains, the learning goes deeper. By allowing and encouraging the student to make up stories that help them to

connect with what they are learning, we are asking them to take the learning personally.

"But what if my student doesn't WANT to do right brain flashcards? What if they learn it just fine without them?"

Well, like I've said before, you are the expert on your child; I'm just here to help you. If you don't want to do right brain flash cards and are absolutely certain your student will not benefit from doing it, then don't. But please give it a whole hearted attempt first.

How to use everyday items as manipulatives

Contrary to popular opinion, you don't need fancy, expensive, and special manipulatives to teach math concepts. What? As shocking as that is, I can personally attest that it is 100 percent true; I've been doing it for years. So how do you turn all those small items that hang around your house and fill your "junk drawer" into useful math manipulatives? Well, let's start with my favorite, the trusty dried bean! When you are teaching your children place value, dried beans just might become your new best friends. How? Simply follow these steps:

When a student is counting 0–9, simply place single beans into the ONES' house, and have the student write the numbers 0–9 on their Place Value Village Mat. As we all know, only 9 ones can live in the ONES' house, so all 9 beans jump out of their house and join up with their new friend, Mr. Tenth bean! They all then jump into a snack-size baggie (usable over and over) and go next door, to live in the TENS' house. Repeat this process, until you have ten baggies of beans trying to live in the TENS' house. Of course, only nine can live there, so all the baggies of ten get traded in for a 100s counter (included in the manipulatives section) and make the move to their new house, the HUNDREDS' house. Dried kidney beans are the best for this, as they are very sturdy! You can also use buttons, paper clips, or basically any small item. They don't even have to be all the same kind of item.

Grading subjective assignments

Most often with math the grading is very objective. For example, 2 + 2 = 4, and no amount of individual expression changes this answer. However, there are times in this course when the answer may depend on a student's reflections of what he or she has learned on a particular day or in a week of assignments. In these subjective cases, the teacher can base a grade for these responses on several more objective measures. Does the student seem to understand the question and answer it as clearly as possible? Does the answer seem complete or does it fail to answer all aspects of the question? So a student may receive full credit if they seemed to meet all the assignment requirements, may get a passing grade if they meet some of the requirements, or may need to repeat the assignment if they didn't meet any of the requirements.

A – Student showed complete mastery of concepts with no errors.

B – Student showed mastery of concepts with minimal errors.

C – Student showed partial mastery of concepts. Review of some concepts is needed.

D – Student showed minimal understanding of concepts. Review is needed.

F – Student did not show understanding of concepts. Review is needed.

Why copywork?

Copywork is widely used in the Charlotte Mason method. I included it in this math curriculum to aid in the learning and reviewing process. However, if you feel like yourmchild is either not yet ready for this amount of writing, or they do not need the practice, please use your own judgement! You are the expert on your child; I am only here to help you.

Tip for young children who are just beginning the process of learning to write: Some children are ready to learn new concepts before they are ready to write them down. This is simply because the small motor skills may develop later than other skills. If your child struggles with writing, try this simple tip. Use a yellow highlighter to write the numbers on the provided lines for your child. Have your child trace them with their pencil.

First Semester Suggested Daily Schedule

Date	Day	Assignment	Due Date	✓	Grade
		First Semester-First Quarter			
Week 1	Day 1	Read Lesson 1 • Pages 15-16 Complete Lesson 1 Exercise 1 • Pages 17-18			
	Day 2	Complete Lesson 1 Exercise 2 • Pages 19-20			
	Day 3	Complete Lesson 1 Exercise 3 • Pages 21-22			
	Day 4	Complete Lesson 1 Exercise 4 • Pages 23-24			
	Day 5	Complete Lesson 1 Exercise 5 **Review Time** • Pages 25-26			
Week 2	Day 6	Read Lesson 2 • Pages 27-28 Complete Lesson 2 Exercise 1 • Page 29			
	Day 7	Complete Lesson 2 Exercise 2 • Pages 30-31			
	Day 8	Complete Lesson 2 Exercise 3 • Page 32			
	Day 9	Complete Lesson 2 Exercise 4 • Pages 33-34			
	Day 10	Complete Lesson 2 Exercise 5 • Pages 35-36			
Week 3	Day 11	Read Lesson 3 • Page 37 Complete Lesson 3 Exercise 1 • Pages 38-39			
	Day 12	Complete Lesson 3 Exercise 2 • Page 40			
	Day 13	Begin Lesson 3 Exercise 3-4 • Page 41			
	Day 14	Finish Lesson 3 Exercise 3-4 • Page 41			
	Day 15	Complete Lesson 3 Exercise 5 **Review Time** • Pages 42-44			
Week 4	Day 16	Read Lesson 4 • Page 45 Complete Lesson 4 Exercise 1 • Page 46			
	Day 17	Complete Lesson 4 Exercise 2 • Page 47			
	Day 18	Complete Lesson 4 Exercise 3 • Page 48			
	Day 19	Complete Lesson 4 Exercise 4 • Page 49			
	Day 20	Complete Lesson 4 Exercise 5 • Pages 50-52			
Week 5	Day 21	Read Lesson 5 • Page 53 Complete Lesson 5 Exercise 1 • Pages 54-56			
	Day 22	Complete Lesson 5 Exercise 2 • Page 57			
	Day 23	Complete Lesson 5 Exercise 3 • Page 58			
	Day 24	Complete Lesson 5 Exercise 4 • Pages 59-60			
	Day 25	Complete Lesson 5 Exercise 5 **Review Time** • Pages 61-62			
Week 6	Day 26	Read Lesson 6 • Page 63 Complete Lesson 6 Exercise 1 • Page 64			
	Day 27	Complete Lesson 6 Exercise 2 • Pages 65-66			
	Day 28	Complete Lesson 6 Exercise 3 • Page 67			
	Day 29	Complete Lesson 6 Exercise 4 • Pages 68-69			
	Day 30	Complete Lesson 6 Exercise 5 **Review Time** • Page 70			

Math Level 2

Date	Day	Assignment	Due Date	✓	Grade
Week 7	Day 31	Read Lesson 7 • Page 71 Complete Lesson 7 Exercise 1 • Page 72			
	Day 32	Complete Lesson 7 Exercise 2 • Page 73			
	Day 33	Complete Lesson 7 Exercise 3 • Page 74			
	Day 34	Complete Lesson 7 Exercise 4 • Pages 75-76			
	Day 35	Complete Lesson 7 Exercise 5 **Review Time** • Pages 77-78			
Week 8	Day 36	Read Lesson 8 • Pages 79-80 Complete Lesson 8 Exercise 1 • Page 81			
	Day 37	Complete Lesson 8 Exercise 2 • Page 82			
	Day 38	Complete Lesson 8 Exercise 3 • Page 83			
	Day 39	Begin Lesson 8 Exercise 4-5 **Review Time** • Pages 84-86			
	Day 40	Finish Lesson 8 Exercise 4-5 **Review Time** • Pages 86-87			
Week 9	Day 41	Read Lesson 9 • Pages 87-88 Complete Lesson 9 Exercise 1 • Page 89			
	Day 42	Complete Lesson 9 Exercise 2 • Page 90			
	Day 43	Complete Lesson 9 Exercise 3 • Page 91			
	Day 44	Complete Lesson 9 Exercise 4 • Page 92			
	Day 45	Complete Lesson 9 Exercise 5 **Review Time** • Pages 93-94			
First Semester-Second Quarter					
Week 1	Day 46	Read Lesson 10 • Page 95 Complete Lesson 10 Exercise 1 **Review Week** • Page 96			
	Day 47	Complete Lesson 10 Exercise 2 **Review Week** • Page 97			
	Day 48	Complete Lesson 10 Exercise 3 **Review Week** • Page 98			
	Day 49	Complete Lesson 10 Exercise 4 **Review Week** • Page 99			
	Day 50	Complete Lesson 10 Exercise 5 **Review Week** • Pages 100-102			
Week 2	Day 51	Read Lesson 11 • Page 103 Complete Lesson 11 Exercise 1 • Page 104			
	Day 52	Complete Lesson 11 Exercise 2 • Page 105			
	Day 53	Complete Lesson 11 Exercise 3 • Page 106			
	Day 54	Complete Lesson 11 Exercise 4 • Pages 107-108			
	Day 55	Complete Lesson 11 Exercise 5 **Review Time** • Pages 109-110			
Week 3	Day 56	Read Lesson 12 • Pages 111-112 Complete Lesson 12 Exercise 1 • Pages 113-116			
	Day 57	Complete Lesson 12 Exercise 2 • Pages 117-118			
	Day 58	Complete Lesson 12 Exercise 3 • Page 119			
	Day 59	Complete Lesson 12 Exercise 4 • Page 120			
	Day 60	Complete Lesson 12 Exercise 5 **Review Time** • Pages 121-124			

Date	Day	Assignment	Due Date	✓	Grade
Week 4	Day 61	Read Lesson 13 • Pages 125-126 Complete Lesson 13 Exercise 1 • Page 127			
	Day 62	Complete Lesson 13 Exercise 2 • Page 128			
	Day 63	Complete Lesson 13 Exercise 3 • Page 129			
	Day 64	Complete Lesson 13 Exercise 4 • Page 130			
	Day 65	Complete Lesson 13 Exercise 5 **Review Time** • Pages 131-132			
Week 5	Day 66	Read Lesson 14 • Pages 133-136 Complete Lesson 14 Exercise 1 • Pages 137-138			
	Day 67	Complete Lesson 14 Exercise 2 • Page 139			
	Day 68	Complete Lesson 14 Exercise 3 • Page 140			
	Day 69	Complete Lesson 14 Exercise 4 • Page 141			
	Day 70	Complete Lesson 14 Exercise 5 • Pages 142-144			
Week 6	Day 71	Read Lesson 15 • Pages 145-146 Complete Lesson 15 Exercise 1 • Pages 147-148			
	Day 72	Complete Lesson 15 Exercise 2 • Page 149-150			
	Day 73	Complete Lesson 15 Exercise 3 • Pages 151-152			
	Day 74	Complete Lesson 15 Exercise 4 • Pages 153-154			
	Day 75	Complete Lesson 15 Exercise 5 • Page 155-156			
Week 7	Day 76	Read Lesson 16 • Pages 157-158 Complete Lesson 16 Exercise 1 • Page 159			
	Day 77	Complete Lesson 16 Exercise 2 • Page 160			
	Day 78	Complete Lesson 16 Exercise 3 • Page 161			
	Day 79	Complete Lesson 16 Exercise 4 • Page 162			
	Day 80	Complete Lesson 16 Exercise 5 • Pages 163-166			
Week 8	Day 81	Read Lesson 17 • Pages 167-169 Complete Lesson 17 Exercise 1 • Page 170			
	Day 82	Complete Lesson 17 Exercise 2 • Page 171			
	Day 83	Complete Lesson 17 Exercise 3 • Page 172			
	Day 84	Complete Lesson 17 Exercise 4 • Page 173			
	Day 85	Complete Lesson 17 Exercise 5 **Review Time** • Page 174			
Week 9	Day 86	Read Lesson 18 • Page 175 Complete Lesson 18 Exercise 1 **Review Week** • Pages 176-177			
	Day 87	Complete Lesson 18 Exercise 2 **Review Week** • Page 178			
	Day 88	Complete Lesson 18 Exercise 3 **Review Week** • Page 179			
	Day 89	Complete Lesson 18 Exercise 4 **Review Week** • Pages 180-181			
	Day 90	Complete Lesson 18 Exercise 5 **Review Week** • Page 182			
		Mid-Term Grade			

Second Semester Suggested Daily Schedule

Date	Day	Assignment	Due Date	✓	Grade
		Second Semester-Third Quarter			
Week 1	Day 91	Read Lesson 19 • Page 183 Complete Lesson 19 Exercise 1 • Page 184			
	Day 92	Complete Lesson 19 Exercise 2 • Page 185			
	Day 93	Complete Lesson 19 Exercise 3 • Pages 186-187			
	Day 94	Complete Lesson 19 Exercise 4 • Pages 188-189			
	Day 95	Complete Lesson 19 Exercise 5 **Review Time** • Page 190			
Week 2	Day 96	Read Lesson 20 • Page 191 Complete Lesson 20 Exercise 1 Review Week • Page 192			
	Day 97	Complete Lesson 20 Exercise 2 Review Week • Page 193			
	Day 98	Complete Lesson 20 Exercise 3 Review Week • Page 194			
	Day 99	Complete Lesson 20 Exercise 4 Review Week • Page 195			
	Day 100	Complete Lesson 20 Exercise 5 **Review Week** • Page 196			
Week 3	Day 101	Read Lesson 21 • Pages 197-198 Complete Lesson 21 Exercise 1 • Page 199			
	Day 102	Begin Lesson 21 Exercise 2-3 • Page 200			
	Day 103	Finish Lesson 21 Exercise 2-3 • Page 201			
	Day 104	Complete Lesson 21 Exercise 4 • Page 202			
	Day 105	Complete Lesson 21 Exercise 5 **Review Time** Pages 203-204			
Week 4	Day 106	Read Lesson 22 • Pages 205-206 Complete Lesson 22 Exercise 1 • Page 207			
	Day 107	Complete Lesson 22 Exercise 2 • Page 208			
	Day 108	Complete Lesson 22 Exercise 3 • Page 209			
	Day 109	Complete Lesson 22 Exercise 4 • Pages 210-211			
	Day 110	Complete Lesson 22 Exercise 5 • Page 212			
Week 5	Day 111	Read Lesson 23 • Pages 213-214 Complete Lesson 23 Exercise 1 • Page 215			
	Day 112	Complete Lesson 23 Exercise 2 • Page 216			
	Day 113	Complete Lesson 23 Exercise 3 • Page 217			
	Day 114	Complete Lesson 23 Exercise 4 • Page 218			
	Day 115	Complete Lesson 23 Exercise 5 **Review Time** Pages 219-220			
Week 6	Day 116	Read Lesson 24 • Pages 221-223 Complete Lesson 24 Exercise 1 • Pages 224-234			
	Day 117	Complete Lesson 24 Exercise 2 • Page 235			
	Day 118	Complete Lesson 24 Exercise 3 • Page 236			
	Day 119	Complete Lesson 24 Exercise 4 • Page 237			
	Day 120	Complete Lesson 24 Exercise 5 **Review Time** • Pages 238-240			

Date	Day	Assignment	Due Date	✓	Grade
Week 7	Day 121	Read Lesson 25 • Page 241 Complete Lesson 25 Exercise 1 **Review Week** • Page 242			
	Day 122	Complete Lesson 25 Exercise 2 **Review Week** • Page 243			
	Day 123	Complete Lesson 25 Exercise 3 **Review Week** • Page 244			
	Day 124	Complete Lesson 25 Exercise 4 **Review Week** • Pages 245-246			
	Day 125	Complete Lesson 25 Exercise 5 **Review Week** • Pages 247-248			
Week 8	Day 126	Read Lesson 26 • Page 249 Complete Lesson 26 Exercise 1 • Pages 250-251			
	Day 127	Complete Lesson 26 Exercise 2 • Page 252			
	Day 128	Complete Lesson 26 Exercise 3 • Pages 253-254			
	Day 129	Complete Lesson 26 Exercise 4 • Pages 255-258			
	Day 130	Complete Lesson 26 Exercise 5 **Review Time** • Pages 249-250			
Week 9	Day 131	Read Lesson 27 • Pages 259-260 Complete Lesson 27 Exercise 1 • Pages 261-262			
	Day 132	Complete Lesson 27 Exercise 2 • Page 263			
	Day 133	Complete Lesson 27 Exercise 3 • Page 264			
	Day 134	Complete Lesson 27 Exercise 4 • Page 265			
	Day 135	Complete Lesson 27 Exercise 5 • Page 266			
		Second Semester-Fourth Quarter			
Week 1	Day 136	Read Lesson 28 • Pages 267-268 Complete Lesson 28 Exercise 1 • Pages 269-270			
	Day 137	Complete Lesson 28 Exercise 2 • Page 271			
	Day 138	Complete Lesson 28 Exercise 3 • Page 272			
	Day 139	Complete Lesson 28 Exercise 4 • Page 273			
	Day 140	Complete Lesson 28 Exercise 5 **Review Time** • Page 274			
Week 2	Day 141	Read Lesson 29 • Pages 275-276 Complete Lesson 29 Exercise 1 • Page 277			
	Day 142	Complete Lesson 29 Exercise 2 • Pages 278-279			
	Day 143	Complete Lesson 29 Exercise 3 • Page 280			
	Day 144	Complete Lesson 29 Exercise 4 • Page 281			
	Day 145	Complete Lesson 29 Exercise 5 **Review Time** • Pages 282-284			
Week 3	Day 146	Read Lesson 30 • Page 285 Gather Materials for a Quilt • Page 286			
	Day 147	Make Your Quilt • Pages 286-288			
	Day 148	Make Your Quilt • Pages 286-288			
	Day 149	Make Your Quilt • Pages 286-288			
	Day 150	Make Your Quilt • Pages 286-288			

Date	Day	Assignment	Due Date	✓	Grade
Week 4	Day 151	Read Lesson 31 • Page 289 Complete Lesson 31 Exercise 1• Page 290			
	Day 152	Complete Lesson 31 Exercise 2 • Page 291			
	Day 153	Complete Lesson 31 Exercise 3 • Pages 292-293			
	Day 154	Complete Lesson 31 Exercise 4 • Page 294			
	Day 155	Complete Lesson 31 Exercise 5 **Review Time** Pages 295-296			
Week 5	Day 156	Read Lesson 32 • Page 297 Complete Lesson 32 Exercise 1 • Page 298			
	Day 157	Complete Lesson 32 Exercise 2 • Page 299			
	Day 158	Complete Lesson 32 Exercise 3 • Page 300			
	Day 159	Complete Lesson 32 Exercise 4 • Page 301			
	Day 160	Complete Lesson 32 Exercise 5 • **Review Time** • Page 302			
Week 6	Day 161	Read Lesson 33 • Page 303 Complete Lesson 33 Exercise 1 **Review Week** • Page 304			
	Day 162	Complete Lesson 33 Exercise 2 **Review Week** • Page 305			
	Day 163	Complete Lesson 33 Exercise 3 **Review Week** • Page 306			
	Day 164	Complete Lesson 33 Exercise 4 **Review Week** • Page 307			
	Day 165	Complete Lesson 33 Exercise 5 **Review Week** • Page 308			
Week 7	Day 166	Read Lesson 34 • Page 309 Complete Lesson 34 Exercise 1 **Review Week** • Page 310			
	Day 167	Complete Lesson 34 Exercise 2 **Review Week** • Page 311			
	Day 168	Complete Lesson 34 Exercise 3 **Review Week** • Page 312			
	Day 169	Complete Lesson 34 Exercise 4 **Review Week** Pages 313-314			
	Day 170	Complete Lesson 34 Exercise 5 **Review Week** • Pages 315-316			
Week 8	Day 171	Read Lesson 35 • Page 317 Complete Lesson 35 Exercise 1 **Review Week** • Page 318			
	Day 172	Complete Lesson 35 Exercise 2 **Review Week** • Page 319			
	Day 173	Complete Lesson 35 Exercise 3 **Review Week** • Page 320			
	Day 174	Complete Lesson 35 Exercise 4 **Review Week** • Page 321			
	Day 175	Complete Lesson 35 Exercise 5 **Review Week** • Page 322			
Week 9	Day 176	Read Lesson 36 • Pages 323-324 Complete Math Opposites • Page 325			
	Day 177	Complete Math Opposites • Page 325			
	Day 178	Complete Math Opposites • Page 325			
	Day 179	Complete Math Opposites • Page 325			
	Day 180	Complete Math Opposites • Page 325			
		Final Grade			

HOW MANY?

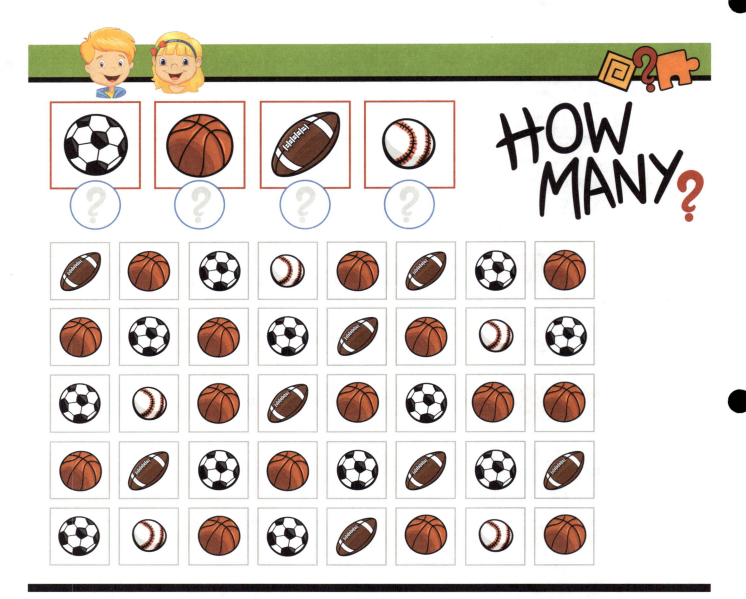

Place Value Village, Telling Time, Shapes and Patterns

It had been a week since Charlie and Charlotte had arrived home from their grandparents' farm. They had experienced such a grand summer with Grandpa and Grandma learning about so many animals, plants, and patterns in nature on the farm. Now that they were home, they were continuing to learn a lot. First off, Mom's round tummy was growing, and they could feel their baby sister kicking from within. Just last night, Charlie had counted 20 energetic kicks, and today, at lunch, Charlotte had counted up to 50 vigorous kicks. Charlie and Charlotte simply could not wait to meet their new little sister! Grandma had explained to them about this wonderful pattern, which God designed, of babies growing securely inside a mother's body while their hearts and lungs grow stronger each day in a warm, safe environment, until they were ready to be born. Knowing God cared so much for their baby sister meant everything to Charlie and Charlotte!

Upon arriving home, Charlie and Charlotte also were excited to discover that Dad had added two new rooms onto their house to create more space for their growing family. The addition consisted of a nursery for the new baby and a schoolroom for Charlie and Charlotte. Filled with hundreds of exciting books and an abundance of art supplies, Charlie and Charlotte could not wait for the school year to begin! Mother had told them they were to start right after Labor Day, which is the first Monday in September. Looking at the new addition, Charlie and Charlotte could not help thinking about Grandpa's Place Value Village. He had shown them the Hundreds' House, the Tens' House, and the Ones' House. Bundling carrots in bundles of 10 with Grandpa and arranging flowers with Grandma in bunches of 10 had helped them understand numbers and place value up to 100. They simply could not wait to add onto their own Place Value Village houses this year!

One more change the twins quickly noticed was that Father had constructed a sturdy-looking pen and shed for Ann and Andy's lambs from Grandpa and Grandma's farm. Nestled snugly in the corner of the yard, in the shape of a rectangle, just like Pokey's bed (Pokey was their pet box turtle), Ann and Andy seemed to already be enjoying themselves as they danced gleefully around in their new home. Every morning at 7:30, right before breakfast, Charlie and Charlotte fed them, and Ann and Andy jumped and skipped happily about.

Although Charlie and Charlotte missed Grandpa and Grandma and the farm, they really were glad to be home. They were extremely excited for school to start, and they could not wait to discover more with Dad and Mom!

Let's begin our adventure together by reviewing counting and place value using our Place Value Village.

Teacher

In preparation for teaching this lesson (and any other lessons about place value), you will need to gather these items:

- At the back of this book, you will find several pages with your "Place Value Village." Please cut out the "houses" and paste each piece on a separate piece of sturdy paper. It would be wise to laminate each "house" to make it more durable.

- For this lesson, gather three cups or containers; a smaller, shorter one (for the ONES' house), a medium one (for the TENS' house), and a larger one (for the HUNDREDS' house); we will add the large THOUSANDS' house later.

- To create your Place Value Village set, adhere your houses onto the side of the containers.

- Also have on hand numerous small items, such as dried beans (kidney beans work very well), 10 snack-size baggies and 9 one-gallon freezer bags.

Place value can be a tricky concept. Please be aware of that this is a concept that your student will grow in for years to come. At this age, and in this book, we are simply laying the foundation for their understanding. Please take time to view the instructional video showing how to set up and use the Place Value Village manipulative.

www.youtube.com/watch?v=fuZ7Y3fDe7c

Count out 20 beans by using your Place Value Village. Write each number on your Place Value Mat.

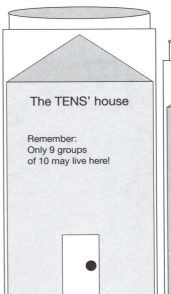

The HUNDREDS' house

Remember:
Only 9 groups
of 100 may live here!

The TENS' house

Remember:
Only 9 groups
of 10 may live here!

The ONES' house

Remember:
Only 9 groups
of 1 may live here!

Copywork:

Teacher

Telling time. If your child has learned to tell time to the hour but is coming into this book after a period of no practice, simply take the time to review the concept. Remind them that the clock shows 12 hours and that the hour hand goes around the face of the clock two whole times in one day. Review the function of the hour hand and the minute hand. Let them study an actual analog clock or watch. Discuss the movements of the hands.

Review Time! Remember, when the short hour hand is pointing directly at a number, and the long minute hand is pointing directly at the 12, we say it is "something o'clock."

Like this:

We say 9 o'clock.

Now it's your turn! Write the time under each clock.

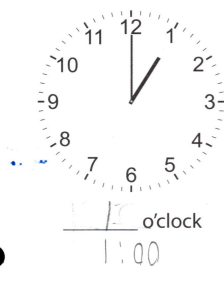  

_____ o'clock   _____ o'clock   ___2___ o'clock

1:00

Copywork:

0   1   2   3   4   5

6   7   8   9   10

11   12   13   14   15

16   17   18   19   20

Patterns and shapes. Deciphering and understanding patterns is foundational to understanding numeric concepts. Please make sure your child understands what patterns are. You may want to encourage your student to point out the patterns in the world around us. For example: the cycles of the seasons, colors of the rainbow, and routines used in their daily life.

Shapes. Have your student name and show you as many kinds of shapes as they can. Encourage them to find objects that depict the shapes. Discuss the difference between squares and rectangles.

Square: four equal sides, four corners that are perfect 90° angles [right angles]

Rectangles: four sides - two longer and two shorter, four corners that are perfect 90° angles [right angles]

The patterns above are made of shapes. What shapes are they?

Tell your teacher what makes a square and then draw one here:

Tell your teacher what makes a rectangle and then draw one here:

If both squares and rectangles have four corners, like this: and four sides that are straight, what is the difference between them?

Copywork:

Practice counting items up to 40 using your Place Value Village.

21 22 23 24 25

21 22 23 24 25

26 27 28 29 30

26 27 28 29 30

31 32 33 34 35

31 32 33 34 35

36 37 38 39 40

36 37 38 39 40

More Shapes.

Discuss the different types of shapes.

Added from last exercise: circles [no corners] and triangles [3 sides]

Color the triangles green, the circle orange, the square blue, and the rectangles red.

Review Time!

Dear Grandma and Grandpa,

We have been having a good time with Mom and Dad since we got back home. We miss both of you so much! How are all the animals? Grandpa, did you harvest all the vegetables yet? Grandma, Mom made us some of your scrumpdelicious oatmeal! We have been practicing all the wonderful math concepts you taught us over the summer. Look how neatly we can write our numbers now!

Copywork:

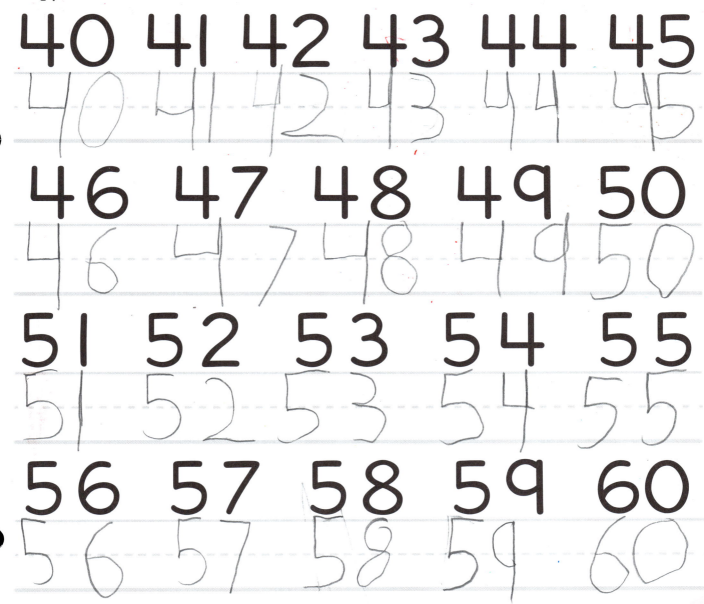

We have been practicing telling time, too! Write the correct time under each clock.

___10___ o'clock   ___7___ o'clock   ___8___ o'clock

Complete the pattern:

Love lots,

Charlie, Charlotte, and our friend, ___Evan___

Addition — Horizontal and Vertical Shapes

Excitement poured out of Charlie and Charlotte as they rushed through their morning chores. Even Ann and Andy seemed more chipper and skipped about inside their pen merrily. Pokey, usually with his head buried in his shell, came out to welcome the twins on this fabulous day, their first day of homeschool! Mom served them a delicious breakfast of chocolate-chip pancakes, sizzling bacon, and freshly squeezed orange juice. Their prayer and devotional time was especially exciting as Dad shared with the twins about the orphanage in South America. Mom and Dad had worked there, during the summer, to help out after a devastating flood.

Dad explained that South America was the continent just south of North America, which is the continent where they lived. Their missionary project for the school year was going to be praying for each orphan at the home and sending them money to help keep the orphanage running. Mom shared with them that an orphan is a child who has no mother or father. The twins could not even imagine how sad they would be without their parents. Dad continued on and told the children that they could each choose a boy and a girl around their own age to specifically pray for all year and to send letters, cards, and gifts to. With eyes full of excitement, the twins felt as if they were adding two more siblings to their family!

After devotions and Bible time, Mom met the children in the schoolroom to begin their first official day of school. Mom began by

Sunday Monday Tuesday Wednesday Thursday Friday Saturday

explaining that this was the month of September, and it was Tuesday. Charlie and Charlotte remembered Grandma teaching them the "Days of the Week" song to the tune of "Row, Row, Row Your Boat" while hanging out laundry, and now they began to sing it for Mom. "Sunday, Monday, Tuesday, Wednesday, Thursday, Friday, Saturday. These are the seven days that make up a week."

Smiling, Mom exclaimed, "That was beautiful, children! And, now we will continue this morning's lessons by designing new flashcards for practicing our addition facts."

The children hurriedly ran to get index cards, markers, and scissors. Mom reminded them of the (+) sign, which stands for "plus", and the (=) sign, which stands for "equals." Charlotte eagerly read the first fact, "One plus one equals two." Next, she wrote it both horizontally and vertically on her flashcard.

"Very nicely done, Charlotte," encouraged Mom.

The children continued working on their flashcards for one-half hour, until Mom called to tell them that it was time for a nature walk. They quickly cleaned up and put away all of their belongings and joined Mom outside, with nature journals and pencils in hand.

Today you are going to create your own flashcards for these facts:

1 + 4 = 5   4 + 1 = 5

2 + 3 = 5   3 + 2 = 5

For those joining our series without completing Book 1, please read the detailed directions for making Right Brain Flashcards in the manipulative section located in the back of this book.

Addition Practice:

Use counting items and your My Addition Mat (both the vertical and horizontal sides) to solve these equations:

2 + 4 = _____   5 + 5 = _____

3 + 5 = _____   4 + 4 = _____

4 + 6 = _____

My equations:

Can you think of more addition facts of your own? Write them below!

As you work your way through this book, you will be creating a calendar. There are 12 months in a year, and you will find a blank calendar page to make copies of in the manipulative section of this book.

Instructions for assembling your very own calendar:

1. Carefully tear the calendar page out. Your teacher will make 12 copies for your calendar.

2. Line up the pages neatly and staple (with your teacher's help) across the top.

3. Each month there will be a reminder to work on your calendar. You may wish to decorate your calendar with stickers or clipart.

A calendar is a chart that shows each month of the year. What month is it right now? Write the name of the month on your calendar. Ask your teacher to help you fill in the numbers for the month that you are in.

Practice saying the days of the week. You will notice that they are "lined up" across the top of your calendar. Talk to your teacher about your calendar. Count the weeks in each one. How many are there?

In a later exercise of this lesson, we will learn the months of the year.

Month _____						
Sunday	Monday	Tuesday	Wednesday	Thursday	Friday	Saturday

Days of the Week. Practice writing the days of the week.

Sunday   Monday

Tuesday   Wednesday

Thursday   Friday

Saturday

Sunday

Monday

Tuesday

Wednesday

Thursday

Friday

Saturday

Addition Practice:

4 + 2 = _____   3 + 3 = _____

6 + 1 = _____   1 + 5 = _____

5 + 5 = _____   3 + 7 = _____

8 + 2 = _____

Use your flashcards to practice your math facts.

3 + 6 = _____   4 + 4 = _____

5 + 3 = _____   5 + 5 = _____

7 + 2 = _____   3 + 3 = _____

Making Time: You will be making your own clock today. Cut out the circle on the dark line. Cut out the hands and attach them to the center of the clock with a brass fastener. Fill in the face of the clock. Carefully write the numbers in.

Teacher *Read note on the back side of this page.*

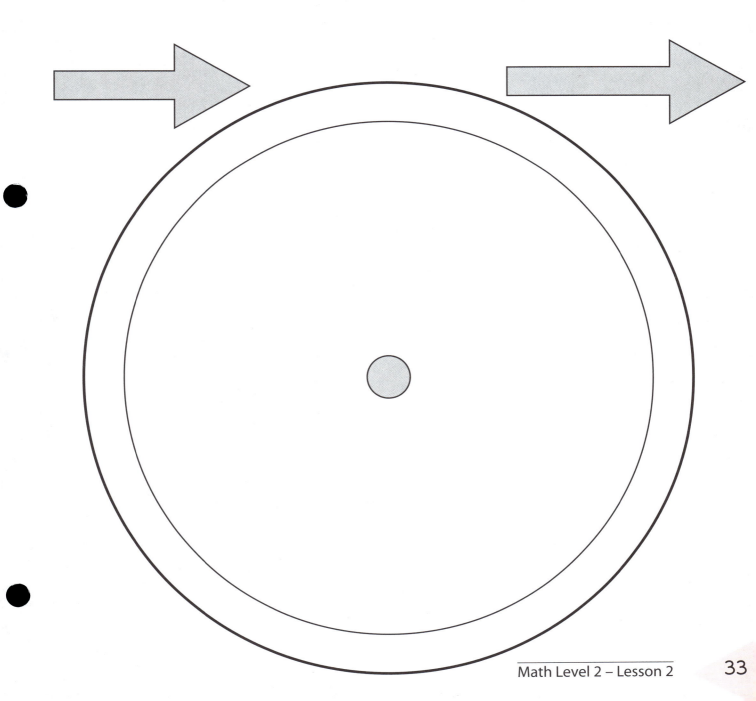

Teacher

This exercise includes a clock that your child can cut out and put together. Even if you own a sturdy plastic manipulative clock, I highly encourage you to have your student put this paper one together. Allowing them to cut it and build it themselves encourages a connection with the concept of telling time.

Do not laminate the clock at this time. We will be adding the minute marks in lesson 13. If you would like to have a sturdier clock for your student to work with, copy the page with the clock onto card stock before cutting it out and assembling it.

Mom wanted to help the children learn the months of the year. A year begins with the month of January. January is followed by February and March, and then comes April, May, June, and July. August follows July, and then comes September, October, November, and December. Begin learning the months of the year by tracing and copying them now.

January

February

March

April

May

June

July

August

September

October

November

December

Now trace and copy the days of the week:

Sunday

Monday

Tuesday

Wednesday

Thursday

Friday

Saturday

Start making flashcards with the days of the week and the months of the year. Make them fun and colorful. Decorate them with pictures and stickers.

Subtraction

The leaves on many of the trees were already beginning to turn brilliant shades of red, orange, and yellow. The birch trees' leaves, still green in color, resembled twinkling jewels, as they fluttered in the gentle autumn breeze, with the bright blue sky overhead. As the twins and Mom strolled along, Mom explained to them that there are two common types of trees: broadleaf trees, which have broad, flat leaves, and conifer trees, which have sharp, narrow leaves, often called needles.

"Many broadleaf trees lose their leaves in the fall and are called deciduous trees. An example of a broadleaf, or deciduous, tree is the maple tree," Mom explained to the children. Continuing, Mom added, "Conifers often are referred to as 'evergreens' because they keep their leaves. Conifers do not grow flowers like broadleaf trees; instead, they have cones, which produce seeds."

"Why do leaves have to fall off the broadleaf trees, Mom?" questioned Charlotte.

"Well, Charlotte," Mom replied, "in the winter, trees cannot take in water due to the ground being frozen. They must survive on the water they have stored in their trunks and branches. Also, in the fall, days get shorter, and thus, there is less sunlight. The leaves need sunlight to make food, so trees will drop their leaves for this reason as well."

"It's kind of like the trees are subtracting their leaves, right, Mom?" asked Charlie, eyes bright with wonder.

"It sure is, Charlie," smiled Mom. "Would you like to go back to the house and begin working on your subtraction flashcards? But, before heading back, why don't you each choose a few leaves for a leaf-rubbing project this afternoon?"

Both children eagerly picked a few different leaves. They could hardly wait to get back home to begin their flashcards and their leaf-rubbing project.

Subtracting is the opposite of adding. When you subtract, the answer you get is smaller than what you started out with. For example:

7 leaves — 3 leaves = 4 leaves

When we subtract, we count backwards, like this:

10, 9, 8, 7, 6, 5, 4, 3, 2, 1, 0

$10 - 1 = $ _____ $5 - 1 = $ _____

$9 - 1 = $ _____ $4 - 1 = $ _____

$8 - 1 = $ _____ $3 - 1 = $ _____

$7 - 1 = $ _____ $2 - 1 = $ _____

$6 - 1 = $ _____ $1 - 1 = $ _____

Numbers for copywork:

10   9   8   7   6   5

4   3   2   1   0

Use your counting items and Larger Subtraction Mat in back to solve some equations. Narrate to your teacher what you are doing. Write (or dictate to your teacher) some of the differences between addition and subtraction.

In the first space in this exercise, allow your child to show you how they understand the concept of how subtraction is different yet related to addition.

In the second space, practice the concept of subtraction by using counting objects and the Large Subtraction Mat in the appendix of the book. (You may also simply use a piece of scratch paper or a white board.) Help your student to write the subtraction equations on the subtraction mat (writing vertically in the one's column) or on the scratch paper or white board, as they complete them. Let them choose a few equations to record in the space in their book.

Time to make more flashcards! Think about what helps you remember your facts. Does making a funny story and drawing silly pictures help? Make your flashcards the way that it will help you! (Take two days to complete this project.)

Use these facts:

$$10 - 1 = 9 \qquad\qquad 10 - 2 = 8$$
$$9 - 1 = 8 \qquad\qquad 9 - 2 = 7$$
$$8 - 1 = 7 \qquad\qquad 8 - 2 = 6$$
$$7 - 1 = 6 \qquad\qquad 7 - 2 = 5$$
$$6 - 1 = 5 \qquad\qquad 6 - 2 = 4$$
$$5 - 1 = 4 \qquad\qquad 5 - 2 = 3$$
$$4 - 1 = 3 \qquad\qquad 4 - 2 = 2$$
$$3 - 1 = 2 \qquad\qquad 3 - 2 = 1$$
$$2 - 1 = 1 \qquad\qquad 2 - 2 = 0$$
$$1 - 1 = 0$$

Create right brain flashcards using the facts in this exercise.

Review Time!

The twins are going to write their grandparents to tell what they have learned about leaves in the fall and how trees "subtract" their leaves until there are none left. Help the twins write their letter by completing the exercises with them. (There is an optional fun project after the letter!)

Dear Grandma and Grandpa,

How are you doing? We are learning so much about so many things! This week Mom taught us about different types of trees and how some of them lose their leaves and some do not. Are the leaves turning beautiful colors at the farm now? When are you coming to visit? Mom and Dad said that you will come help take care of us when Mom has our new baby sister. We can't wait to see her . . . and you!

This week we have been learning about subtraction. We are learning all of these facts!

$10 - 1 = 9$	$5 - 1 = 4$	$10 - 2 = 8$	$5 - 2 = 3$
$9 - 1 = 8$	$4 - 1 = 3$	$9 - 2 = 7$	$4 - 2 = 2$
$8 - 1 = 7$	$3 - 1 = 2$	$8 - 2 = 6$	$3 - 2 = 1$
$7 - 1 = 6$	$2 - 1 = 1$	$7 - 2 = 5$	$2 - 2 = 0$
$6 - 1 = 5$	$1 - 1 = 0$	$6 - 2 = 4$	

Subtraction is like counting backwards! Like this: (Write the numbers 10-0 without looking back at previous pages.)

Love, Charlie, Charlotte and our friend, _____.

How to do a colorful leaf rubbing:

Choose a sturdy leaf. The best leaves for this project are broadleaf such as sugar maple. Place the leaf under the paper and gently rub a crayon over the entire surface. You will see the shape of the leaf coming through. For the best results, peel the paper off of the crayon and use the entire side of the crayon instead of just the tip.

Teacher *Encourage your student to complete this exercise as independently as possible. Enjoy the leaf rubbing project!*

My leaf rubbing:

Writing Numbers to 100, Simple Fractions

Wow! The twins could not believe it! The month of September was flying by. Today was a cloudy, rainy day, and the children were helping Mom with many projects around the house. She needed to finish a sewing project that she had been working on for the children in the orphanage. She had been very busy sewing a stuffed toy for each child. Now, at the end of the project, all Mom had left to do was to sew on the eyes. She needed 100 buttons to finish up. Charlie and Charlotte were very eager to help by counting out 100 buttons, which would be the eyes for the stuffed toys. They used their Place Value Village houses to count the buttons.

The twins practiced counting numbers to 100 with their Place Value Village. This week you will be using your Place Value Village to count items up to 100.

Today, use your items to count to 25 and write the numbers on your Place Value Counting Mat. Leave the numbers on your mat; you will be adding to it over the next few days. Narrate to your teacher what you are doing. When you are finished, copy the numbers on the lines. (Try to write them from memory!)

Teacher

Exercises 1 through 4

Practice working with the Place Value Village. As your child works through these exercises, please remember that place value is a concept that grows with practice and developmental growth. Be patient and encouraging.

Today, use your items to count from 26 through 50 and write it on your Place Value Counting Mat. Copy the numbers here.

Today, use your items to count from 51 through 75 and write it on your Place Value Counting Mat. Copy the numbers here.

Today, use your items to count from 76 through 100 and write it on your Place Value Counting Mat. Copy the numbers here.

After Mom taught the twins how to sew on the buttons (eyes) and they were busy at work, she began to make an apple pie in the kitchen. Soon, the delicious aroma of apple pie filled the house. Charlie and Charlotte, upon finishing their sewing project, ran into the kitchen to check on the pie. Spying it cooling on the countertop, Charlie exclaimed, "I am so hungry I could eat the whole pie, Mom!"

"Well, it does need to cool off a bit before I cut it," said Mom, "and then you may have a fraction of the pie, Charlie."

"While it cools, could we review fractions, Mom?" asked Charlotte, remembering Grandma's lessons on fractions.

"Sure," answered Mom.

As Mom began explaining true fractions as being equal parts of a whole, Charlie's mouth watered for Mom's delicious apple pie. Usually loving these learning opportunities, Charlie was just too hungry to pay attention well. Realizing this, Mom decided to use the cooled pie to review fractions with the children. Cutting the pie in half, Mom explained that this was the fraction one-half, which is written like this: $\frac{1}{2}$. Next, she cut each half of the pie in half, making four pieces of pie; she explained this was the fraction one-fourth, which is written like this: $\frac{1}{4}$. Finally, Mom cut each one-fourth of the pie in half, making eight pieces of pie in all. Charlie grabbed plates, forks, and napkins, and Charlotte scooped one piece of pie onto each plate.

While the twins eat their pie, let's practice our fractions.

Teacher

Explore the concept of true fractions with your student. Explain to them that a true fraction has perfectly equal parts. Have your student fold a piece of paper in "half" with uneven parts. Have them explain to you why they are not true halves. (One part is bigger/smaller than the other.) Now have them practice folding a piece of paper as suggested at the bottom of the page.

Color the true fractions. Remember that true fractions are equal parts of the whole. Color the $\frac{1}{2}$ green. Color the $\frac{1}{4}$ blue.

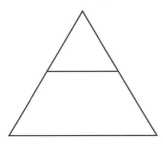 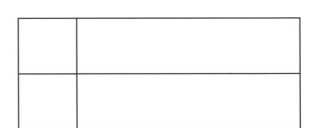 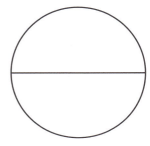

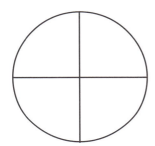 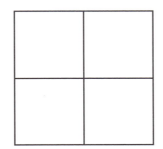 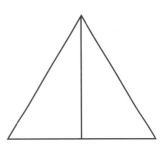

Here is a project to help understand fractions. Cut out a square of paper. Remember, a square has four equal sides and four corners which are right angles. Fold your square in half, then in half again. Now you have a half and a quarter!

flat, square piece of paper   fold in half   fold in half again

 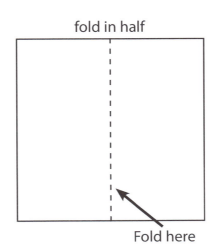 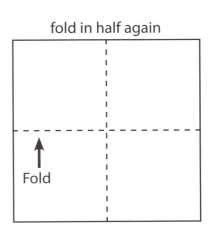

Fold here

Fold

Match each fraction with its proper visual image. The numbers above the line in these fractions are shown in red. The first one is done for you.

Introducing Word Problems

As Charlie and Charlotte turned the calendar, they were excited to see that it was now October. The days were definitely shorter, and it was getting cooler. The autumn leaves were vibrant with color, and many leaves had dropped off the trees and were, as the twins discovered, great fun to play in. Ann and Andy enjoyed romping in the leaf piles as much as tbohe twins did. Pokey really enjoyed basking in the sun on his rock on these sunny autumn days.

"Mom," asked Charlotte, as they were out on another fall stroll, "why do leaves change color?"

"Well," replied Mom, "as the days are getting shorter, there is less sunlight. The leaves need lots of sunlight to make their food. In the fall, due to shorter periods of daylight and cooler temperatures, the leaves stop their food-making process. In their cells, there is a pigment called chlorophyll, which gives the leaf its green color. Since the chlorophyll gets its energy from sunlight and aids the leaf in the food-making process, and we now have less sunlight, the chlorophyll breaks down and the green color disappears, exposing colors of yellow, orange, and red in the fall."

"That is another wonderful pattern in nature, isn't it, Mom?" asked Charlotte.

"It sure is, dear," replied Mom, "and now, do you children want to each pick ten of the most beautiful leaves you can find to do a project with later on?"

"Yay! Yippee! Another project!" exclaimed the very enthusiastic children.

The twins are learning that sometimes there are math equations in life around them. For example, they know that their family has 4 members right now, and when their baby sister is born, there will be 1 more. They learned how many members their family will have all together by adding 4 and 1 to find 5.

This kind of "math problem" is called a word (or story) problem. It is important to know how to solve word problems. When you know how to solve them, you can have fun finding and solving problems all around you!

These are the steps to solve a word problem:

1. Read the problem carefully.

2. Ask "what is the question?"

3. Circle the numbers you will need to use to solve the problem.

4. Think it through. Will you need to add or subtract? There are key words or clue words that will tell you what you need to do. If your word problem has the words "all together," you know you will need to add, because adding will tell you what everything together is. If your word problem has the words "what is the difference," you know you will need to subtract. Subtracting will tell you how much more or less one number is than another. Underline these words.

5. The last step is to think about your answer to see if it makes sense.

Just like everything else in life, learning to solve word problems takes practice! We will start by working it out in steps. Use counting items if you need to.

Word Problem 1:

After the twins cleaned up their room, they counted their toys. Charlie had 4 toy trucks, and Charlotte had 3 dolls. How many toys did the children have all together? Fill in the numbers and solve the problem. Narrate to your teacher what you are doing.

_____ trucks + _____ dolls = _____ toys all together

Word Problem 2:

The twins were going to have a baby sister soon! They were so excited to hold her and count her little fingers and toes. They knew that she would have 5 fingers on one hand and 5 more on the other tiny hand. How many tiny, sweet, baby fingers would their little sister have all together?

_____ little fingers + _____ more little fingers = _____ all together

Word Problem 3:

The twins' mom had been carrying their baby sister all safe and warm inside of her for 8 months. Mom told them that she had 1 more month before the baby was due to be born. How many months all together would Mom carry their baby sister?

_____ months + _____ months = _____ months all together

Word Problem 4:

When the twins came home from their grandparents' farm, they discovered that Dad had built an addition on their house! Before, their house had contained 8 rooms. They were excited to find out that there were 2 more rooms: a nursery for the baby and a brand-new, beautiful schoolroom just for them! How many rooms does their house have all together?

_____ rooms + _____ rooms = _____ rooms all together

Did you follow the five steps with each problem?

Review!

Write the correct time under each clock.

_____ o'clock

_____ o'clock

_____ o'clock

_____ o'clock

_____ o'clock

_____ o'clock

Today we are going to practice more word problems. We are going to practice problems using subtraction. In subtraction word problems, we look for the words "what is the difference," "how many were left," or "how many more?" Just like in all subtraction problems, you start with the large number and take away the smaller number.

Word Problem 1:

Charlie and Charlotte were helping Mom clear the table after lunch. There were 4 plates on the table. Charlie took 2 to the sink. How many were left for Charlotte to carry?

_____ plates - _____ plates = _____ left over

Word Problem 2:

Mom said she was going to carry the twins' new baby sister for 9 months. She had already carried her for 8 months. How many months were left?

_____ months - _____ months = _____ months left

Word Problem 3:

When Mom and the twins brought out the fall clothes at the end of the summer, they found that Charlie had outgrown 5 pairs of jeans, and Charlotte had outgrown 4 winter tops. How many more articles of clothing had Charlie outgrown than Charlotte?

_____ jeans - _____ tops = _____ more that Charlie had outgrown

Word Problem 4:

When the twins first saw their new schoolroom, they were so excited! They spent a whole hour looking at all the new and wonderful books and projects their parents had placed there. They also discovered 8 new containers of brightly colored modeling clay. After asking permission, they used 5 containers to make gifts for Grandma and Grandpa. How many containers were left?

_____ containers - _____ containers = _____ containers left

Today, you get to make up your own word problems! With your teacher's help, look around your home or classroom. Write or dictate to your teacher your word problems in the spaces below. Use the steps in Exercise 1 to solve your word problems.

My Word Problems ✏️

Word Problem 1:

Word Problem 2:

Use your flashcards to drill your addition and subtraction facts.

Now try solving these word problems. Circle the numbers and any words that will help you solve the problems. Solve in the space below each problem.

Word Problem 1:

When the twins were on their nature walk with Mom, they found 6 red leaves and 3 orange leaves on their front yard. How many leaves did they find all together?

Word Problem 2:

Charlie decided to use all orange leaves for his project, but Charlotte loved the golden leaves. There were 10 orange leaves in a pile on Charlie's desk, and 7 golden leaves on Charlotte's desk. How many more leaves does Charlie have than Charlotte?

Word Problem 3:

Mom combined her pile of 5 red leaves to a pile of 4 orange leaves. How many leaves does Mom have all together?

Word Problem 4:

When Dad came home from work that day, he announced that the leaves he found on lunch break were the most beautiful he had ever seen! They came from an oak tree by the front door of the house Dad is helping to build. The leaves that he placed on the table were almost golden honey colored! There were 9 large ones and 6 smaller ones. How many more large leaves than small leaves are there from the oak tree?

Review Time!

Divide these shapes into equal fractions. Make two $\frac{1}{2}$ and two $\frac{1}{4}$. Color the $\frac{1}{2}$ orange and the $\frac{1}{4}$ red.

Review Time!

Dear Grandma and Grandpa,

We are so excited! This week we learned something brand new . . . word problems! Mom and Dad taught us that there are word problems all around us every day. So far we have learned story problems using addition and subtraction.

Like this: (Solve these word problems.)

In nature study today, we learned why trees lose their leaves during the fall. Charlie picked up 8 bright red leaves and 3 yellow leaves. How many more red leaves are there than yellow leaves?

We helped Mom fold towels and sheets today. We folded 8 sheets and 2 towels. How many did we fold all together?

This is one we made up! (Write or dictate your own word problem.)

Love lots!

Charlie, Charlotte, and our friend,

Name_____

Connect the Dots.

Skip Counting by Using Dimes and Nickels, Minutes on the Clock

Charlotte and Charlie were so very excited! They had been saving their dimes and nickels for their "adopted" brother and sister in South America. Today they were going to the bank to cash their dimes and nickels in for dollar bills, so they could send Hairo and Natalia a little gift.

Mom was explaining to them that a dime is worth ten cents and they could write it like this: 10¢. The ¢ sign stood for "cents" just like the (+) sign stood for "plus" in an addition problem. Also, Mom explained that since a dime is worth 10¢, they could count by tens to add the dimes up. Charlie and Charlotte remembered Grandpa and Grandma teaching them to count by tens using their Place Value Village. Each number, when counting by tens, ends in 0, like this:

0, 10, 20, 30, 40, 50, 60, 70, 80, 90, 100

With their dimes, the twins could just add the ¢ sign each time like this:

0¢, 10¢, 20¢, 30¢, 40¢, 50¢, 60¢, 70¢, 80¢, 90¢, 100¢

"100¢ equals one dollar, children," explained Mom, "and there are ten tens in every one hundred, and so if every ten dimes is equal to 100¢, then every ten dimes is also equal to one dollar bill from the bank."

Trace the cent signs:

¢ ¢ ¢ ¢ ¢ ¢ ¢ ¢ ¢

Now write some of your own:

Charlie and Charlotte quickly began counting their dimes out into piles of ten and counted each pile up to 100¢. Practice counting these dimes. Write the amount.

_____ ¢

_____ ¢

_____ ¢

_____ ¢

_____ ¢

Numbers for copywork:

10 20 30 40 50

60 70 80 90 100

"Now children," said Mom, "we need to count the nickels. Nickels are worth five cents, and so we need to count by fives now."

"I love counting by fives!" announced Charlie, with much enthusiasm, "Grandpa taught us how to do that. Every number we say has to end in a '0' or a '5', like this: 0, 5, 10, 15, 20, 25, 30, 35, 40, 45, 50, 55, 60, 65, 70, 75, 80, 85, 90, 95, 100."

"Well done, Charlie," encouraged Mom, "and now with nickels, what do you suppose we do?"

"I know, I know," chipped in Charlotte, "we just add a ¢ sign to the end of each number, and when we get to 100¢, that is another dollar bill from the bank."

"Very good, Charlotte," said Mom with a smile.

Charlie and Charlotte excitedly began to count and separate their nickels into piles of 100¢ by counting by fives to 100.

After counting by tens and by fives, the twins realized they would receive six one-dollar bills for their dimes and two one-dollar bills for their nickels to help their friends at the orphanage. They were so excited!

Practice counting the nickels. Remember to count by 5s!

_____¢

_____¢

_____¢

Counting by fives copywork:

5   10   15   20   25

30   35   40   45   50

55   60   65   70   75

80   85   90   95   100

Now let's review both!

On the lines below, write the numbers you say when you count by 10s:

_____

_____

  a nickel is worth _____ ¢.

  a dime is worth _____¢.

Count the dimes out loud to your teacher. _____¢

Use your flashcards to drill your addition and subtraction facts.

The twins could not wait to get to the bank! Mom told them they would leave in approximately 20 minutes.

"How long is 20 minutes, Mom?" Charlotte asked, forgetting how time telling worked.

"I will explain it to you after we get home from the bank," responded Mom, "okay?"

"All right Mom, thank you," said Charlotte.

At the bank, a very helpful lady, known as a bank teller, assisted the twins in the recounting of their dimes and nickels, and then counted out eight one-dollar bills into their awaiting hands. The twins couldn't wait to get home and begin to work on cards for Hairo and Natalia to include with their gifts of money for them.

After their adventure at the bank, Mom remembered her promise to help Charlotte with time-telling. Mom sat down at the table with the twins and began by drawing a circle and asking them how many minutes are in one hour. They remembered Grandpa and Grandma telling them that there are 60 minutes in one hour. Each number on the clock, 1–12, represents 5 minutes, like this:

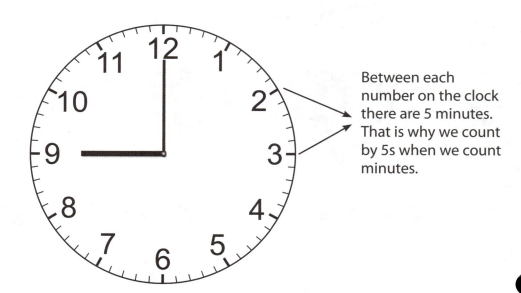

Between each number on the clock there are 5 minutes. That is why we count by 5s when we count minutes.

By counting by 5s, we can see that there are 60 minutes in one hour.

It all began coming back to Charlotte now. She remembered Grandma teaching her and Charlie about the clock and how the hour hand goes around the clock two whole times in one day. She also remembered that the first time the hands go around is known as a.m., or morning, and the second time they go around is p.m., or afternoon and evening.

Use your clock to count the minutes by 5s. Narrate to your teacher what you are doing. Write the minutes by 5s around the clock. The first two are done for you.

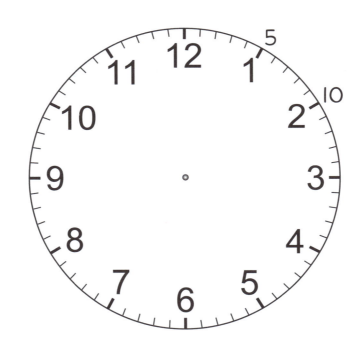

Fill in the missing numbers counting from 0 through 60 by 5s.

0, _____, 10, 15, _____, 25, _____, _____, 40, 45, _____, _____, _____

Review Time! Check each one off as you do it.

☐   Use your My 100s Chart to count by 5s and 10s.

☐   How much is a dime worth? _____¢

☐   How much is a nickel worth? _____¢

☐   Use your flashcards to drill your addition and subtraction facts.

☐   Narrate to your teacher everything you know about telling time.

☐   Solve these word problems:

Charlie had a nickel, which he knew was worth 5¢. Charlotte gave him another nickel, which was another 5¢. How much does Charlie have all together?

The twins counted 10 coins before they gave their mom 3 for the baby's piggybank. How many coins do they have left?

Skip Counting by 2, Review Even and Odd Numbers

Skipping down Main Street toward the post office, Charlie and Charlotte excitedly held onto their letters for Hairo and Natalia. They each had written them a letter to include with a gift they were sending.

The postmaster examined the address and then weighed each envelope on a scale. He then punched in the zip code for the city of Lima in Peru in South America and told the children and Mom what it would cost. As Mom handed him the money for postage, the postmaster put stamps on the envelope and set them in a pile of other letters.

As they exited the post office, Mom pointed out a group of school-aged children walking with their teacher in groups of two. That, of course, reminded Charlie of skip-counting by twos, and he began to count the children — 2, 4, 6, 8, 10, 12, 14, 16, 18, 20, 21.

"Mom, there is an odd guy out," exclaimed Charlie, "there is not another guy for him to walk two-by-two with."

Mom smiled at Charlie's enthusiasm and teachable spirit, and she responded, "Twenty-one is an odd number, Charlie. Any number ending in 1, 3, 5, 7, or 9 is said to be odd, and any number ending in 0, 2, 4, 6, or 8 is said to be even."

"So," Charlie said with a teasing grin on his freckled face, "our family is even right now with four of us, but when our new baby comes, we will be odd with five."

Their mother smiled and responded, "But no one in our family will be an 'odd guy out.'"

And with that, the three chuckled merrily and headed over to the ice cream parlor for their favorite treat in town.

The twins and their mother practiced counting by 2. Do you remember the story of Noah's ark, and how many of the animals entered the ark walking in groups of 2? Let's practice! Trace the numbers and fill in the missing numbers counting by 2 from 0 through 20.

0, ____, 4, 6, ____, 10, ____, ____, 16, 18, ____

What pattern do you see? Look at the last digit in each number and narrate to your teacher the pattern the 2s make.

Mom told the twins that numbers that end in these numbers are called even numbers. This means that this number of items can be separated into groups of 2 and have nothing left over at the end. Use your counting items to make groups.

Count out the following number of items and separate them into groups of 2. Check the box if you can make groups of 2 with no "odd guy out" left over. Do not check the box if there is an "odd guy out." Narrate to your teacher what you are doing.

☐ 1 item   ☐ 3 items   ☐ 5 items   ☐ 7 items   ☐ 9 items
☐ 2 items   ☐ 4 items   ☐ 6 items   ☐ 8 items   ☐ 10 items

Write the even numbers here:

_____

- -

_____

Write the odd numbers here:

_____

- -

_____

In our last exercise, we learned about even and odd numbers. Even numbers always end in 0, 2, 4, 6, and 8. It does not matter how big a number is; if the last digit is one of these numbers, it is an even number.

Look at this number and ask your teacher to read it to you: **4,684**

Look at the last digit of this big number. Is it one of the even numbers? Yes! So if you had that big, big number of items and a big, big amount of time, you could separate the items into groups of 2 and have no odd guy out! Aren't numbers fun?

Now ask your teacher to read this number for you: **6,549**

Look at the last digit. Is it one of the even numbers? No! So, again, if you had that big, big number of items and a big, big, big amount of time, you could separate the items into groups of 2 . . . and there would be an odd guy out!

Numbers for copywork:

0   1   2   3   4   5

6   7   8   9   10

11   12   13   14   15

Circle each of the last digits and say them out loud.

Super Challenge!

Write a big number here _____. Challenge another student or your teacher to read the number. Did you write an even number or an odd number? _____ How do you know? _____

_____

Make a big pile of counting items on the table or your desk. Look at your pile but don't count the items yet! Guess how many items you have in your pile. Write your guess here: _____. Now count your items. How many? _____ Is it an even or odd number? _____ How do you know? _____

_____

Write the even numbers here: _____, _____, _____, _____, _____

Write the odd numbers here: _____, _____, _____, _____, _____

Write the age of everyone in your family. Check the even box if their age is an even number, or check the odd box if their age is odd. Use the extra space on the right if you run out of room.

_____   ☐ even   ☐ odd

_____   ☐ even   ☐ odd

_____   ☐ even   ☐ odd

_____   ☐ even   ☐ odd

_____   ☐ even   ☐ odd

_____   ☐ even   ☐ odd

Use your My 100s Chart to find all the numbers that are even. Remember, all you have to do is count by 2! Place a counting item or, if your chart is laminated, color in each number with a washable marker. Do you see the pattern?

Now use your 100s Chart to find all the numbers that are odd. If your chart is laminated, color them in. All the odd numbers you just colored on your chart end in these numbers: 1, 3, 5, 7, 9.

Narrate to your teacher what an even number is and what an odd number is.

Show and Tell!

Use your counters to show what you have learned about even and odd numbers. Ask your teacher to take a picture of your show and tell. Paste a couple in the space below and on the next page. Write or dictate to your teacher some of what you learned in this lesson.

Exercise **4** Day **34**

Show and Tell! (continued)

Review Time!

Dear Hairo and Natalia,

We are writing this letter to tell you about something very exciting! Mom said that we may write you letters every week.

Have you started school yet? Mom and Dad told us about the new school building at the orphanage. It sounds wonderful! We go to school right in our own home. It is a lot of fun! We have already learned so many new things.

Do you know what even and odd numbers are? Mom explained it to us this way. All even numbers end in these numbers: 0, 2, 4, 6, 8. When a number is even, you can divide that group into smaller groups of 2 with nothing left over. When a number is odd, it ends in one of these numbers: 1, 3, 5, 7, 9

Like this:

Take the following number of items and make groups of 2. Are there any "odd guys out?" Write odd or even next to the number.

22 _____   38 _____

13 _____   18 _____

29 _____

All even numbers end in: _____

All odd numbers end in: _____

The trees in our front yard have lost all of their leaves in preparation for winter. We can't wait for the snow to come!

Love,

Charlie, Charlotte, and our friend _____.

Find the missing answers by adding or subtracting.

Addition — Double Digit Plus Single Digit

Sitting at the kitchen table with their Place Value Village spread out before them, Charlie and Charlotte looked at Mom with inquisitive faces and asked her how to add bigger numbers to smaller numbers. Mother removed the Hundreds' House for now and set the Tens' House and Ones' House in front of them. She took some numbered cards and set a "1" in the Tens' House and another "1" in the Ones' House.

"What number is this, children?" she asked.

"Why, it's eleven, Mom" responded Charlotte, "one 'ten' and one 'one' is 11."

"Nicely done, Charlotte," encouraged Mom.

Next, Mom added a "5" in the Ones' House under the "1." She then asked Charlie, "Now how many 'ones' do I have?"

Charlie excitedly responded, "Why, you have six ones now, Mom. I know! I know! I know! You have one 'ten' and six 'ones' so now you have sixteen, so we can say that 11 + 5 is equal to 16, right, Mom?"

"Yes, Charlie, yes, you are right," smiled Mom, trying her best not to explode with laughter over her son's contagious enthusiasm.

Charlotte eagerly asked, "Mother, will you please give me an addition problem with bigger numbers now?"

"Sure, Charlotte," replied Mom.

Mom removed the numbers in the Tens' House and in the Ones' House and now placed a "2" in the Tens' House and a "5" in the Ones' House. She placed a "3" under the "5" in the Ones' House and then glanced at Charlotte, "Okay, Charlotte, what do you think?"

Charlotte's blue eyes sparkled as she began talking it out, "Well, we have to look in the Ones' House first. We have five 'ones' plus three more 'ones.' That makes eight 'ones.' We have two 'tens' so that makes '28' for the answer. So, Mother, 25+3=28."

"You are correct, Charlotte! Very good job!" exclaimed Mom. "And you are right. We always need to look at the Ones' House first and add them up, and then we can look at the Tens' House."

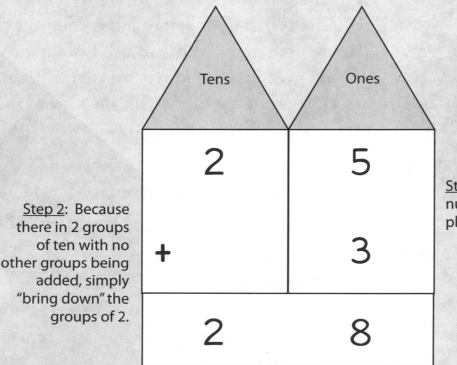

Step 2: Because there in 2 groups of ten with no other groups being added, simply "bring down" the groups of 2.

Step 1: Add the numbers in the ONEs' place first.

Mother showed them the way they would write the problems on paper, like this:

$$\begin{array}{r} 25 \\ + 3 \\ \hline 28 \end{array}$$

With eyes twinkling, the twins continued working on bigger number addition problems for the next hour. Mom smiled contentedly and continued knitting the blanket for their new baby, who was, at this very moment, kicking enthusiastically from within her.

Let's practice with these addition problems. Use your "Larger Addition Mat" in the back of the book, and counting items. If you like, you can remove it and laminate it, then use washable markers.

$$\begin{array}{r} 90 \\ +\ 8 \\ \hline \end{array} \qquad \begin{array}{r} 61 \\ +\ 5 \\ \hline \end{array} \qquad \begin{array}{r} 80 \\ +\ 6 \\ \hline \end{array}$$

$$\begin{array}{r} 53 \\ +\ 4 \\ \hline \end{array} \qquad \begin{array}{r} 33 \\ +\ 5 \\ \hline \end{array} \qquad \begin{array}{r} 24 \\ +\ 5 \\ \hline \end{array}$$

Clock Practice:

Fill in the face of the clock and draw hands to show the correct time.

7 o'clock

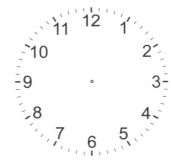
3 o'clock

8 o'clock

12 o'clock

It's important to practice the new concepts as we learn them. Solve these addition problems. Remember to add the ones' column first. Use your counting items.

$$
\begin{array}{r} 90 \\ +\ 8 \\ \hline \end{array}
\qquad
\begin{array}{r} 84 \\ +\ 5 \\ \hline \end{array}
\qquad
\begin{array}{r} 72 \\ +\ 2 \\ \hline \end{array}
$$

$$
\begin{array}{r} 24 \\ +\ 4 \\ \hline \end{array}
\qquad
\begin{array}{r} 56 \\ +\ 2 \\ \hline \end{array}
$$

Use your flashcards to drill your facts.

☐ Addition

☐ Subtraction

Solve these addition problems. Remember to add the ones' column first. Use your counting items.

```
  53        73        93
+  2      +  6      +  1
_____     _____     _____
```

```
  56        63
+  3      +  5
_____     _____
```

Complete these patterns. Circle the next shape.

_____

_____

Review Time!

Today and tomorrow, use your Place Value Village Counting Mat and counting items to solve these problems. Solve five problems each day and choose one review activity. Narrate to your teacher what you are doing.

$$\begin{array}{r} 52 \\ +\ 7 \\ \hline \end{array} \qquad \begin{array}{r} 61 \\ +\ 3 \\ \hline \end{array} \qquad \begin{array}{r} 32 \\ +\ 4 \\ \hline \end{array}$$

$$\begin{array}{r} 23 \\ +\ 5 \\ \hline \end{array} \qquad \begin{array}{r} 81 \\ +\ 7 \\ \hline \end{array} \qquad \begin{array}{r} 92 \\ +\ 4 \\ \hline \end{array}$$

$$\begin{array}{r} 91 \\ +\ 5 \\ \hline \end{array} \qquad \begin{array}{r} 74 \\ +\ 2 \\ \hline \end{array} \qquad \begin{array}{r} 51 \\ +\ 6 \\ \hline \end{array}$$

$$\begin{array}{r} 64 \\ +\ 4 \\ \hline \end{array}$$

Review Activities:

Solve these word problems. Remember to follow the steps.

Charlie loves ice cream! Last week he ate a cone which had 2 scoops of ice cream, and this week, he ate a cone which had 2 scoops. How many scoops of ice cream has Charlie eaten all together?

Charlotte is practicing jumping rope. On Monday, she jumped 10 times without stopping, and on Tuesday she jumped 9 times without stopping. How many times did Charlotte jump all together?

Practice counting these coins.

_____ ¢

_____ ¢

_____ ¢

Write how many kids are in each picture, then on the bottom add them all up.

 + + +  =

Addition - Double Digit Plus Double Digit

Perched atop a hay wagon on the way to pick apples at their favorite orchard, Dad, Mom, Charlie, and Charlotte smiled enthusiastically at each other as the wagon bumped along through the woods. Most of the deciduous trees were bare now, having lost almost all of their leaves. They were all wearing warmer clothing, as temperatures were decreasing each day. Nights were becoming quite chilly, and they even had experienced frost once already.

"I can't wait to pick apples!" exclaimed Charlotte. "I am so thankful that we are here. Thank you for bringing us, Mom and Dad."

"Yes, thank you, Dad and Mom," chipped in Charlie.

"You are so welcome, children," responded their father. "Now, remember, you each get to pick 21 apples today. Look for apples without blemishes and bruises, okay, children?"

"Okay," the children responded energetically.

As the wagon came to an abrupt halt, Charlie, Charlotte, and their parents retrieved their picking bags and were off to find the most scrumptious-looking apples on the trees. Dad demonstrated the proper way to get apples off of the trees, by twisting the apple at the stem, and not by just yanking them off and possibly causing damage to the trees. Charlie and Charlotte listened attentively, and then each began filling their bags with 21 choice apples.

After their picking was finished, and the wagon returned them to the orchard store to pay for their delicious fruit, the family sat down at a picnic table and devoured a scrumptious lunch of chicken salad sandwiches on freshly made bread, Mom's homemade potato salad, coleslaw, and very yummy chocolate-chip oatmeal cookies.

"Yum, that was deeeeeeeeeeeeeeelicious!!" exclaimed Dad as he wiped his face with a napkin and then stretched his long arms out.

"Yes, it definitely was!" agreed Charlie.

Dad then pulled out a notebook and pencil, drew a Tens' House and Ones' House, put a "2" in the Tens' House and a "1" in the Ones' House, and then he put another "2" in the Tens' House and another "1" in the Ones' House, like this:

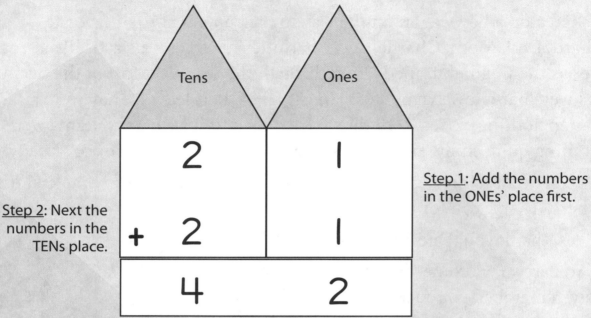

Step 1: Add the numbers in the ONEs' place first.

Step 2: Next the numbers in the TENs place.

"Now," Dad asked, "how many apples did you two pick all together?"

"Well," Charlie responded, "we have one 'one' plus one 'one' in the Ones' House, so that makes two 'ones.'"

Charlotte jumped in, "And we have two 'tens' plus two 'tens' in the Tens' House, and that makes four 'tens.'"

"So, altogether we have four 'tens' plus two 'ones' and that equals 42, right, Dad?" Charlie could hardly contain his excitement right now.

"Yes, Charlie and Charlotte," replied Dad, "well done!"

Dad then showed the twins how double digit addition looked on paper, like this:

$$\begin{array}{r} 21 \\ +\ 21 \\ \hline 42 \end{array}$$

What an incredibly perfect day this was! The twins were absolutely loving all the new things they were learning, and Dad and Mom were so thankful that Charlie and Charlotte were so quickly grasping these new concepts.

Now it's your turn to try. Talk with your teacher as you work through these problems. Remember to add the ones' column first.

$$41 + 21$$ $$43 + 42$$ $$65 + 34$$

Numbers for copywork:

0   2   4   6   8   10

12   14   16   18   20

5   10   15   20   25

30   35   40   45   50

More Addition Practice.

$$\begin{array}{r} 86 \\ +\ 12 \\ \hline \end{array} \qquad \begin{array}{r} 53 \\ +\ 24 \\ \hline \end{array} \qquad \begin{array}{r} 41 \\ +\ 21 \\ \hline \end{array} \qquad \begin{array}{r} 76 \\ +\ 13 \\ \hline \end{array}$$

Review even and odd numbers.

On your My 100s Chart, point to each even number as you say it out loud. What numbers do each of the even numbers end in? Write them here:

On your My 100s Chart, point to each odd number as you say it out loud. What numbers do each of the odd numbers end in? Write them here:

More Addition Practice.

$$
\begin{array}{r} 71 \\ +\ 10 \\ \hline \end{array}
\qquad
\begin{array}{r} 84 \\ +\ 11 \\ \hline \end{array}
\qquad
\begin{array}{r} 67 \\ +\ 31 \\ \hline \end{array}
\qquad
\begin{array}{r} 55 \\ +\ 33 \\ \hline \end{array}
$$

☐   Practice addition and subtraction flashcards

☐   Practice months of the year flashcards

☐   Narrate to your teacher the months of the year without looking at your flashcards.

Narrate to your teacher what you have learned about adding larger numbers. Solve the following problems.

$$\begin{array}{r} 96 \\ +\ 2 \\ \hline \end{array} \qquad \begin{array}{r} 33 \\ +\ 33 \\ \hline \end{array}$$

Count the Money.

_____ ¢

When you count dimes, you count by _____.

_____ ¢

When you count nickels, you count by _____.

☐   Larger Addition Mat: If you feel that your student could use a little more practice, use your Larger Addition Mat from the appendix to practice the concept being taught in this exercise. This can be laminated or slipped into some type of page protector. The use of this mat is optional. Simply use it to give your child extra practice in the concept being taught in the lesson.

Review Time!

Show what you learned about adding larger numbers. Use these addition problems to show them.

$$\begin{array}{r} 93 \\ +\ 6 \\ \hline \end{array}$$
$$\begin{array}{r} 62 \\ +17 \\ \hline \end{array}$$

Count your practice money to show what you have learned about counting dimes and nickels.

How many dimes did you count? _____

How many cents were there together? _____

How many nickels did you count? _____

How many cents were there together? _____

Count how many are in each group of objects or people. Put the number of the first group in the first circle. Put the number of the second group in the next circle. Then solve the problem and put the answer in the last circle.

Addition Review — All Concepts Learned

The next morning, Charlie and Charlotte awakened to the wonderful aromas of freshly brewed coffee, sizzling bacon, and their favorite — Swedish pancakes! After making their beds and getting dressed in record time, they raced down the stairs to tackle their chores quickly, in order to sit down and enjoy this delectable feast! Upon entering the kitchen, they were greeted by their grandparents instead of their parents.

"Good morning, Charlie and Charlotte," Grandpa said, with a twinkle in his eyes.

Charlotte, with a huge smile on her face, exclaimed, "Hi, Grandpa and Grandma! You must be here because our new little sister is going to be born. Mom told us you would be coming to watch us when the baby came."

"Yes, Charlotte, your mother went into labor last night while you and Charlie slept. Your parents had called us yesterday and let us know that the time was near. They are at the hospital right now, and after breakfast, Grandpa and I will take you to meet this sweet little addition to our family," Grandma said with a smile.

The scrumptious breakfast smells were fading fast from the twins' memories now, as they were so very eager to get to the hospital and meet their new sister. "Can we go now . . . pleeeeeeeeease?" the twins begged.

"No, we will go as soon as we eat and the chores are done. Your mother and little sister are resting right now, anyway," Grandpa responded, smiling at his grandchildren's delightful enthusiasm.

While Charlie and Charlotte are visiting their mother and baby sister at the hospital, we are going to take some time to review all the new concepts we have learned over the last few weeks.

Review Time!

Check off each one as you complete it.

☐ Use counting items to count out 50 items. Narrate to your teacher what you are doing.

How many groups of 10 do you have? _____

How many groups of 1 do you have? _____

☐ Explain to your teacher the difference between adding and subtracting. Why are they opposite? (Orally narrate to your teacher the answers to these questions.)

☐ Practice your addition and subtraction facts using your flashcards.

☐ Write the numbers 0–100 on the blank side of your My 100s Chart.

Review Time!

Check off each one as you complete it.

☐ Cut circles, squares, rectangles, and triangles out of construction paper (2 each). Divide half of them into halves by drawing a line with your ruler and cutting them to make 2 equal parts. (**Tip:** ask your teacher to check your line before you cut to make sure it is equal.) Divide the remaining shapes into quarters by following the same procedure.

☐ In the space below, write and solve two word problems. Make one an addition problem and one a subtraction problem.

#1

#2

☐ Using your money manipulatives, count out the following amounts:

50¢ (use dimes) How many dimes did you use? _____

75¢ (use nickels) How many nickels did you use? _____

Review Time!

Check each one off as you complete it.

☐ Count out the following numbers of items. Decide if they are even or odd. Circle odd or even.

9   odd   even

12   odd   even

24   odd   even

17   odd   even

6   odd   even

21   odd   even

Even numbers end in: _____, _____, _____, _____, _____

Odd numbers end in: _____, _____, _____, _____, _____

☐ Narrate to your teacher everything you have learned about odd and even numbers.

Review Time!

Check each one off as you complete it.

☐   Use your Larger Addition Mat to work these out. Narrate to your teacher what you are doing. Tell what you remember about adding larger numbers.

$$\begin{array}{r} 80 \\ +\ 6 \\ \hline \end{array} \qquad \begin{array}{r} 90 \\ +\ 8 \\ \hline \end{array} \qquad \begin{array}{r} 61 \\ +\ 5 \\ \hline \end{array}$$

$$\begin{array}{r} 24 \\ +\ 5 \\ \hline \end{array} \qquad \begin{array}{r} 53 \\ +\ 4 \\ \hline \end{array} \qquad \begin{array}{r} 33 \\ +\ 5 \\ \hline \end{array}$$

☐   Using your money manipulatives, count out 7 dimes. _____¢

☐   Count out 15 nickels. _____¢

Review Time! Solve these word problems.

Word Problem 1:

Grandma and Grandpa are going to stay for 10 days to help take care of the twins after Mom had their baby sister, Ella. After that, Grandpa is going back home to the farm, but Grandma is staying for another 10 days. Grandma is going to stay for how many days all together?

Word Problem 2:

Charlie and Charlotte helped their dad build shelves in the baby's room in preparation for Ella's arrival. They built 5 shelves on one wall and 10 more in the closet. How many more shelves were in the closet than on the wall?

Divide these shapes into halves.

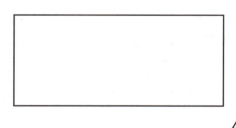 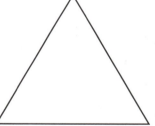 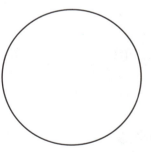 

Divide these shapes into quarters.

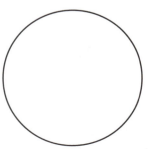  

Name______________________________

Exercise 5 Day 50

Trace the days of the week and say them out loud:

Sunday

Monday

Tuesday

Wednesday

Thursday

Friday

Saturday

Good job!

How many circles
are here?
Count only those
that have the entire
circle visible.
For example, 1,
and not 2.

Ella was amazing! From the downy, blonde fluff on the top of her precious, little head to the ten tiny, pink toes adorning her soft, adorable feet, the twins could not believe just how enchanting their new little sister was. Just this morning, at the hospital, Charlie and Charlotte had each been able to snuggle and hold baby Ella! She was so soft and cuddly. Charlotte thought she was especially adorable when she would yawn, and her tiny mouth would open wide in the shape of an oval. Charlie wondered at Ella's petite fingers and the way she would grasp and hold onto his finger with her own little hand. Grandma found her baby-soft, silky skin to be incredible! Everyone agreed that Ella was a precious addition to their family.

After lunch, the doctor stopped in to check on Mom and Ella. He had been delighted to announce to the twins that Ella measured 22 inches long and weighed eight pounds and four ounces. After the doctor left, Dad explained to Charlie and Charlotte that 12 inches equals one foot. He grabbed a ruler out of the twins' bag, which they had packed with all sorts of interesting items to keep them occupied at the hospital. Dad showed them that the ruler measured 12 inches long. He further explained that Ella, being 22 inches long, was not quite two feet tall, because two feet is 12 inches plus 12 inches, or 24 inches.

While the twins were scampering around the room measuring all sorts of objects, baby Ella began to fuss. Mom was quick to check her diaper and change her. Ella continued to fuss and then started to cry louder. Mom had explained to Charlie and Charlotte that when Ella was hungry, had a wet or messy diaper, or was in pain, crying was the only way she could communicate. She wouldn't be able to talk for a long time, and crying was not only a way for her to communicate but a fantastic way to exercise her lungs as well.

Mom began to feed Ella, and she quieted down at once. The twins could not believe how often their baby sister would eat and how long she would sleep after that! It seemed to them that she ate every two hours or so! Mom explained to them that this was God's design too. Babies need to sleep and eat a lot in the first few weeks in order to continue growing stronger each day!

Dad explained to the children that 12 inches = 1 foot. Let's explore this concept a little further. Use your ruler to answer these questions (this may be completed orally).

☐   Is each inch the same as all the rest?

☐   Spread your hand open as far as you can. How wide can you spread it?

☐   Measure your math book. How many inches wide is it?

☐   Measure these items. How many inches is each one?

- your pencil
- your teacher's hand
- your foot
- your arm

Use your ruler to measure these lines. Write how many inches long each one is.

_____ _____ inches

_____ _____ inches

_____ _____ inches

_____ _____ inches

Review: Fill in the blanks counting by 5s.

_____, 5, _____, _____, 20, _____,

30, _____, 40, 45, _____, 55

Remember that when we count minutes, we can count by 5s. Use your clock and practice counting the minutes. Narrate to your teacher what you are doing.

Using your ruler and a pencil, draw lines from the star for the lengths listed below.

5 inches ☆

2 inches ☆

6 inches ☆

4 inches ☆

Practice your addition facts using your Addition Fact Sheet from the back of this book. You can laminate it so you can use it over and over.

Use your clock to work out these word problems.

Ella ate at one o' clock this afternoon. She eats again in three hours. What time will it be? _____

Charlie and Charlotte eat dinner at six o' clock. They go to bed two hours after that. What time is their bedtime? _____

Dad gets up at five o' clock in the morning. He leaves for work one hour later. What time does Dad leave for work? _____ He arrives home from work nine hours after he leaves. What time will it be? _____

Mom goes to bed at ten o' clock every night after feeding Ella. She gets up seven hours later. What time does Mom get up in the morning? _____

Review

$$23 \atop + 46$$ $$15 \atop + 34$$ $$73 \atop + 26$$ $$58 \atop + 21$$

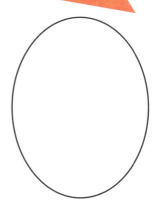

When Ella opened her sweet, little mouth to yawn, her mouth opened in the shape of an oval. An oval is kind of like a stretched-out circle. It looks like this:

In the space provided, practice drawing a circle, a square, a triangle, a rectangle, and an oval.

Circle:

Square:

Triangle:

Rectangle:

Oval:

Use different colors of construction paper, cut out shapes to make a pattern, using at least three of the shapes you practiced drawing.

Practice your subtraction facts using your Subtraction Fact Sheet from the back of the book. You can laminate it so you can use it over and over.

Review Time!

Now that Ella and Mom were resting quietly, Charlie and Charlotte decided to write a letter to their friends in South America! It was November, and they had lots of exciting news to share, including the safe arrival of their new little sister. Maybe they would even send some photographs of Ella for them to see.

Grabbing colored pencils and paper they had brought, the twins were occupied for the next hour writing letters and drawing pictures for their friends thousands of miles away.

Dear Hairo and Natalia,

Hola! How are you doing? We have some really exciting news to share with you. Our baby sister, Ella, joined our family recently. She is so adorable. We are at the hospital meeting her today. She looks like this:

Besides meeting our new little sister, we have also been learning all sorts of interesting things in homeschool. We have learned a lot about telling time, adding and subtracting larger numbers, and solving word problems. We also have learned how to measure using inches. Ovals are the new shape we have learned; ovals look like stretched-out circles. We understand that you are learning many things in your school, too. Here are some of the things we have been learning.

This is an oval.

Dad showed us how to measure using a ruler. Here is a line that is 5 inches long.

 ——————————————————————————

It is 3:00 (three o' clock) right now. We are leaving the hospital in two hours with Grandpa and Grandma. What time are we leaving?

_____

Here is a picture of an American dime and nickel.

Well, we sure look forward to hearing from you guys. We will write again soon.

Sincerely,

Charlie, Charlotte, and our friend, _____

Introducing Perimeter

Home from the hospital with Ella a couple of days later, Charlie and Charlotte and their parents and grandparents busily began preparing for Thanksgiving. Grandpa had explained to the twins that the first Thanksgiving had taken place in 1621 in Plymouth in New England. Seeking religious freedom, the Pilgrims were a group of people who had come to the United States in 1620. The first winter had been incredibly tough for the Pilgrims and many died. In the spring, an Indian named Squanto, and some of his Indian friends, showed the Pilgrims how to grow corn, beans, squash, and pumpkins. Together, in the fall of of 1621, the Pilgrims invited over 90 Indians to a feast to give thanks. Later, Grandpa explained that President Abraham Lincoln had officially named the fourth Thursday of November as Thanksgiving Day.

Looking forward to Thursday with much anticipation, Charlie and Charlotte were busily making colorful name cards for each place at the table. They were so excited that Grandpa and Grandma were able to stay and join them for Thanksgiving. In fact, Grandpa had promised them that later on they would do a special project with him in the garage. Finishing up the place cards, the twins cleaned up their mess and trotted off to find Grandpa.

Grandpa was deep in concentration when they found him in the garage at the workbench, looking at a pile of various-sized boards.

"Hi, children," Grandpa said with a twinkle in his eyes.

"Hi, Grandpa!" the children replied in unison, "What are we going to make?"

"Well," Grandpa answered, "we need something to feed the birds all winter long. Since you have been feeding them this fall, they rely on you to continue through the winter.

"Either we need to stop feeding them so they can fly south now or we need to make a feeder for them, so they have enough food for the winter and then they won't die from lack of food."

"We sure don't want our pretty birds dying!" Charlie exclaimed, "We are making a bird feeder, right, Grandpa?"

"Yes, Charlie, we sure are," Grandpa chuckled, wondering once again at the children's enthusiasm.

Grandpa and the twins spent the rest of the afternoon working on cutting out the pieces for two bird feeders. Grandpa explained to the children how important it was to measure every piece correctly before cutting it out with the saw. Charlie and Charlotte were so tickled to help Grandpa out and keep the beautiful birds safe throughout the approaching winter months.

Teacher

The perimeters of the following shapes will not all be exact in measurement. For example, for the sake of the problem, it might say 4 inches but actually be $3\frac{1}{2}$ inches on a side. Please explain this to your students if they have their rulers out and are measuring with them.

Perimeter is the distance around a polygon. A polygon is simply a shape made with straight sides. "Poly" is a prefix which means "many"; thus, a polygon is a shape with many straight sides. To figure out the perimeter of a rectangle, we just need to add up each side, like this:

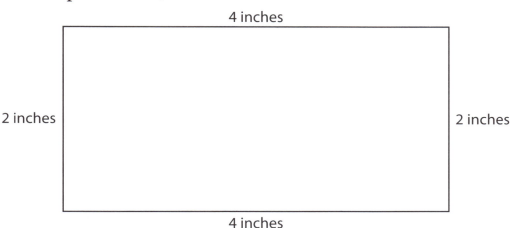

4 inches

2 inches   2 inches

4 inches

☐   First, add the shorter sides together:

2 inches + 2 inches = 4 inches

☐   Next, add the longer sides together.

4 inches + 4 inches = 8 inches

☐   Last, add the totals together:

8 inches + 4 inches = 12 inches

So the perimeter of this rectangle is 12 inches.

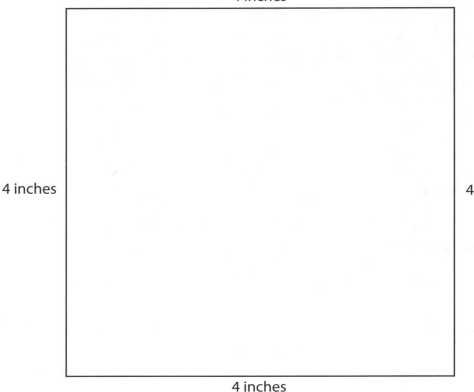

For a square, add two sides together, and then add the other two sides together. Now, take those two numbers and add them together to find the perimeter.

4 inches + 4 inches = 8 inches

4 inches + 4 inches = 8 inches

8 inches + 8 inches = 16 inches

So the perimeter of this square is _____ inches.

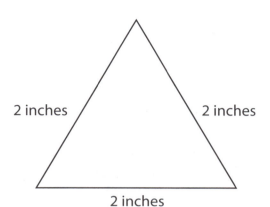

2 inches   2 inches

2 inches

To figure out the perimeter of a triangle, add two sides together. Now, add that number to the other side, and you will find the perimeter. By the way, some triangles have equal sides, while other triangles have unequal sides.

2 inches + 2 inches = 4 inches

4 inches + 2 inches = 6 inches

So the perimeter of this triangle is _____inches.

Count the nickels and write how many cents.

_____ ¢

What did you count by to come up with your answer?

Count the dimes and write how many cents.

_____ ¢

What did you count by to come up with your answer?

Calculate the perimeter of the following polygons, following the steps you learned in our last lesson.

3 inches

1 inch   1 inch

3 inches

_____ + _____ = _____

_____ + _____ = _____

_____ + _____ = _____

_____ inches

2 inches

2 inches   2 inches

2 inches

_____ + _____ = _____

_____ + _____ = _____

_____ + _____ = _____

_____ inches

3 inches   3 inches

4 inches

_____ + _____ + _____ = _____

_____ inches

Draw hands on the clocks to show the right time.

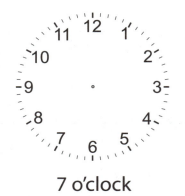

7 o'clock

12 o'clock

3 o'clock

In working with perimeter today, we will be doing a hands-on activity. We will use construction paper, scissors, a pencil, and a ruler. Measure and cut out the following shapes, and then figure out the perimeter for each.

☐ One square with 3-inch sides: _____ inches

☐ One triangle with 5-inch sides: _____ inches

☐ One rectangle with two 3-inch sides and two 6-inch sides: _____ inches

☐ One square with 7-inch sides: _____ inches

☐ One triangle with a 1-inch side and two 6-inch sides: _____ inches

☐ One rectangle with two 2-inch sides and two 4-inch sides: _____ inches

☐ For this last project today, use all the figures you have cut out, and make a giant picture. You may add in circles and ovals to complete your picture. Show it to your class or family, and share with them what you have learned about perimeter and measuring.

Addition:

$$23 + 46 \qquad 15 + 34 \qquad 73 + 26 \qquad 58 + 21$$

☐ Use your flashcards to review addition and subtraction facts.

Figure out the perimeter of the following shapes. Notice that you will be adding with some double digits today.

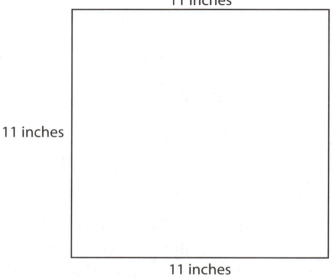

11 inches

11 inches   11 inches

11 inches

_____ + _____ = _____

_____ + _____ = _____

_____ + _____ = _____

_____ inches

11 inches

1 inch [   ] 1 inch

11 inches

_____ + _____ = _____

_____ + _____ = _____

_____ + _____ = _____

_____ inches

8 inches   8 inches

2 inches

_____ + _____ + _____ = _____

_____ inches

Review Time!

To solve the following word problems involving perimeter, first draw the figure on another piece of paper, and label each side. Next, figure out the perimeter using the steps taught earlier in the lesson.

We have a rectangle with two 6-inch sides and two 8-inch sides. What is the perimeter?

We have a triangle with one side that is 4 inches, one side that is 3 inches, and one side that is 5 inches. What is the perimeter?

We have a square with 7-inch sides. What is the perimeter?

Just for Fun!

Have you ever had a bird feeder or a birdhouse? Charlie and Charlotte are so excited to feed the birds all winter long. You don't have to have a bird feeder to feed the birds. There are many other ways to feed the birds all year long. One of them includes decorating a tree for the birds using dried fruit, birdseed, peanut butter, popcorn, and old bagels and bread. Listed on the next page are some ideas for you.

Wildlife Energy Muffins

You will need:

1 cup chunky peanut butter

1 cup pure rendered suet or vegetable shortening

$2\frac{1}{2}$ cups coarse yellow corn meal

Seeds, raisins, or other dried fruit and roasted peanuts

Pipe cleaners

1. Mix peanut butter, suet, and corn meal together. Stir in seeds, fruit, and nuts.
2. Make "muffins" by placing the mixture into a muffin tin. Sprinkle seeds on top.
3. Place a pipe cleaner in each muffin to act as a hanger, and place the tin in the freezer to harden.
4. Once hardened, hang the muffins from a tree.

Bagels for the Birds

You will need:

1 bag of bagels (old, stale ones work best)

1 jar of plain peanut butter

1 bag of birdseed

1 roll of ribbon (cloth or gift wrapping ribbon)

1. Split bagels lengthwise, and let them harden overnight. Tie lengths of ribbon through each bagel hole.
2. Spread peanut butter over both sides of each bagel slice.
3. Sprinkle with birdseed.
4. Hang bagels throughout your backyard.

Use this page to create a "Backyard Bird-Watching Journal" of your very own. Your teacher has permission to make as many copies as you need. Have a bird field guide for your state or area handy, to identify the birds that come to your yard.

 (A picture or drawing of the bird I saw.)

Where I saw it: _____

What kind of bird is it? _____

What kind of food does it like? _____

Describe it:

How many triangles
are here?
Count only those
that have the entire
shape visible.
For example,
1, and not 2.

Telling Time to the Minute

Thanksgiving Day had been filled with special memories. Mom and Grandma had prepared a delicious feast for all to enjoy. Everyone had taken turns holding precious, little Ella, and they had played many board games all afternoon.

Charlie and Charlotte's favorite memory from the day was when each shared what they were most thankful for. Of course, everyone agreed they were most thankful that God had given Ella a safe arrival and that she was doing so well adjusting to life outside of the womb. Charlie also shared how thankful he was for school; he just loved learning about everything. Charlotte agreed with Charlie and added that she especially was grateful for parents and grandparents who were so eager to teach them. Dad and Mom were thankful for children who were such enthusiastic students and also for a warm, cozy home. Grandpa and Grandma had felt very blessed to be with their family for this wonderful holiday.

DECEMBER

Now it was December and, to the twins, December meant winter was coming and even more exciting, Christmas was around the corner! So far, only snow flurries had fallen, but one of these days, they would have the first official snowfall. Today, Charlie and Charlotte were diligently working on their December calendars, drawing a manger scene with baby Jesus, shepherds, Mary, Joseph, and lots of animals. Mom and Dad read the Christmas story to them every year and explained to them that Christmas was the day to celebrate Jesus' birthday.

"Children," Mom interrupted their glorious thoughts of Christmas, December, and Jesus' birthday, "when you have finished your calendars, please come out here."

"Okay, Mom," they replied in unison.

Completing their calendars a few minutes later, they joined Mom in the living room, where she had their clocks on the table.

"Today, children, we will be learning how to tell time to the minute," Mom explained, "we have learned about telling time to the 5s and 10s and today we will learn the rest. As I told you previously, there are 60 minutes in an hour. Each line on the clock represents one minute." Mom now demonstrated how to add the "minute lines" to their clocks.

In preparation for the new time-telling concepts we will be learning in tomorrow's exercise, you will be reviewing counting to 60 by 1s and 5s. You will need your 100s Chart for this exercise.

On the blank side of your chart, fill in the numbers by 1s up to 60. Now, with a different color of marker, circle all the numbers that you say while counting by 5s. Write all the numbers you circle on the lines below.

Use your flashcards to review your math facts. Are there any facts that you are still having a hard time remembering? Write them here and make sure you practice those more often.

Use the clock that you assembled in Lesson 2 of this book. Today you will be adding the individual minute marks on the clock. Remember that each number on the clock stands for 5 minutes.

After you have completed writing the minute marks on your clock, start at 3 o'clock and practice moving the minute hand minute by minute around the clock. This is the way we write the time to the minute:

3:00

3:01

This clock shows exactly 3 o'clock, which is written 3:00. The two zeros after the ":" means that it is "0 minutes" after the hour of 3.

This clock show the minute hand has moved past the 12 mark by 1 minute. This means that it is now 3:01.

This 0 shows 1 minute has passed since 3:00. This 0 holds the place until it becomes 3:10. When writing time, always remember that there must be two digits after the ":".

Study the following clocks.

3:05

3:08

3:09

Charlie, Charlotte, and Mom were occupied for quite a long while, working with their clocks and quizzing each other using them. What fun it was to be able to tell time!

Today we will practice using the clock to tell time to the minute. Use your clock to show your teacher these times. Check them off as you do them.

☐   5:21

☐   3:46

☐   1:10

☐   2:09

☐   12:11

☐   10:45

☐   6:30

☐   8:27

☐   11:17

☐   2:05

☐   7:01

☐   9:52

☐   4:03

☐   3:48

Addition practice:

| 19 | 23 | 22 | 52 |
| + 40 | + 46 | + 33 | + 47 |

| 91 | 72 | 54 | 65 |
| + 5 | + 7 | + 3 | + 23 |

Measure the lines. Write the length in inches on the lines.

_____

_____

_____

_____

_____

_____

Review Time!

Review place value. Use your Place Value Village to count out the following amounts. Narrate to your teacher what you are doing.

☐   35

☐   78

☐   22

☐   46

☐   81

☐   54

Show your teacher what you have learned about telling time to the minute. Using your clock, show them these times:

☐   10:19

☐   4:06

☐   11:32

☐   6:02

☐   9:07

☐   4:24

If we have a square that is 10 inches on each side, what is the perimeter? Remember the steps. _____ inches

Charlie wanted to make a card for Grandma. He cut a rectangle out of construction paper that was 7 inches long on two sides and 5 inches long on the other two sides. What was the perimeter of his card? _____ inches

Telling the time

1. **I wake up at** _____

2. **I take a shower at** _____

3. **I have breakfast at** _____

4. **I have dinner at** _____

5. **I go to bed at** _____

Place Value Village Practice — Place Value to the Thousands' Place

Charlie and Charlotte were thrilled. When they woke up this morning, they were greeted, upon looking out their window, by white, fluffy snowflakes. They were so excited they could barely get their beds made and race downstairs.

"Mom, Dad, guess what?" Charlie shouted, "It's snowing! It's snowing!"

Mom and Dad, smiling at their son's engaging enthusiasm, motioned for the twins to sit down for breakfast.

"It has been snowing most of the night, children," replied Dad, "and right after breakfast and devotions, you may go out and feed Ann and Andy and then play in the white, fluffy snow."

"Yay!" exclaimed the twins together, excitement filling them from the tops of their heads to the bottoms of their stocking feet.

During a scrumptious breakfast of fried eggs and baked oatmeal with strawberries, Dad shared between bites, "Children, do you know that every single snowflake is different? Each has its own unique shape. However, all snowflakes have six sides or points, but they form millions of different patterns. Snowflakes are made when it gets so cold that the water in a cloud freezes and then turns to ice."

"Wow, Dad, that is so cool!" Charlie responded with wide eyes.

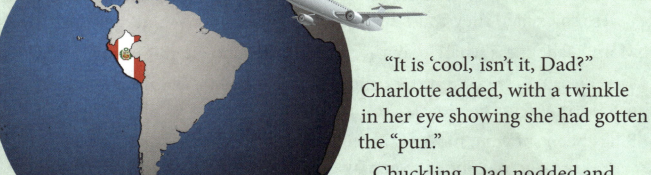

"It is 'cool,' isn't it, Dad?" Charlotte added, with a twinkle in her eye showing she had gotten the "pun."

Chuckling, Dad nodded and then took his Bible from the shelf to begin devotions. During prayer time, Dad brought up their friends in South America at the orphanage.

"How far is it to Peru, Dad?" Charlotte inquired.

"Why, it's thousands of miles away, Charlotte! We would need to fly in an airplane if we ever have the opportunity to visit Hairo and Natalia," Dad responded.

"How many is 'thousands,' Dad?" asked Charlotte, eager to understand even bigger numbers.

"Well," replied Dad, "Later, after you two munchkins play in the snow, we will build a 'Thousands' House' to add to your Place Value Village, and I will help you learn how to count in bigger groups and learn bigger numbers."

"Thanks, Dad!" Both children were now eagerly anticipating both the fun-in-the-snow time and later learning about even larger numbers than they already knew. After cleaning the table, the twins raced away to locate their snow pants, boots, wool socks, hats, mittens, and winter coats in the entryway. Minutes later, they were outdoors, head-to-toe covered in snow. During the next couple of hours they made snow angels, played "Fox and Geese," rolled snowballs, had a snowball fight, and made a snowman.

Mom handed them a carrot for the nose, they found two black rocks for the eyes and a few more for the mouth, and a couple of dead branches for the arms. Lastly, they wrapped an old scarf around his neck and topped off their snowman with one of Dad's old hats. What an incredibly delightful morning!

With pink noses and cheeks, they returned to the house, hung up their wet snow clothes, and joined Dad and Mom in the kitchen for some hot chocolate. Baby Ella, strapped in her baby swing, was rocking gently next to them.

While Mom prepared lunch, Dad brought out the Place Value Village with the new Thousands' House and began explaining to the twins how, as numbers have more digits, we continue adding houses to the village, like this:

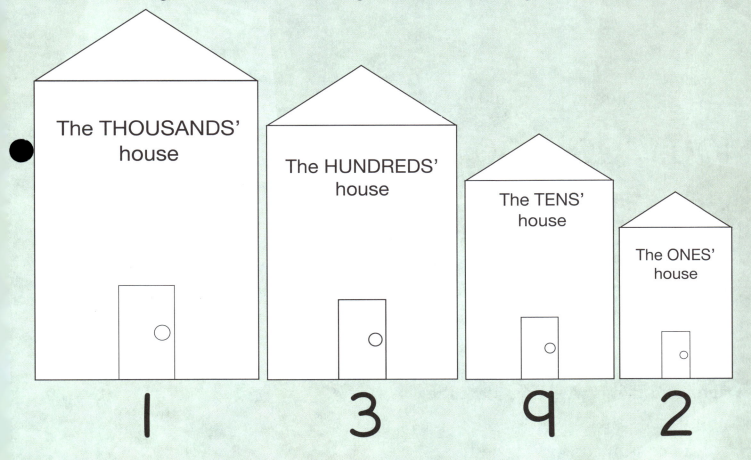

"This number is read 'one thousand, three hundred, ninety-two.'" Dad explained. "That means, we have 2 ones, 9 tens, 3 hundreds, and 1 thousand. There are 10 sets of one hundred in one thousand, just as there are 10 sets of 10 in one hundred and 10 ones in each 10.

We can count by sets of 100 to 1,000, like this:

100, 200, 300, 400, 500, 600, 700, 800, 900, 1,000

"Also, when we have more than three digits, like the example 1,392, we need a comma in our number," Dad further instructed. "A good way to know where the comma goes is to count from the right-side digit, in this case, the '2.' Count three digits from the right, and that is where we place the comma, like this: 1,392."

Dad continued working with the twins until lunch was ready. He assured them they could spend as much time as they needed in order to understand this new place concept.

value

Practice counting by 100s.

Numbers for copywork:

100 200 300 400 500

600 700 800 900

Read and discuss the following concepts with your teacher.

When you have a large amount of items to count, it is easier to put them into groups of 10 to count them. When you have groups of 10, you can easily count by 10s. Like this:

10, 20, 30, 40, 50, 60, 70, 80, 90, 100.

When you have a very large amount of items to count, if you can make groups of 100, you can count them easily by counting by 100s. Like this:

100, 200, 300, 400, 500, 600, 700, 800, 900.

Up until now, we have learned place value by counting items up to 100 using counting items and our Place Value Village. Because 1,000 is a big number made up of 10 groups of 100, we cannot count items for it. For example, if we had 100 beans, we could easily count them. When we have 1,000 beans, we would have 10 bags of 100 beans each! That would take you all day to count, and it would be easy to make a mistake! Now that we are adding the Thousands' House to our Place Value Village, you are going to use a special set of counting manipulatives from the back of this book. Take time right now to find and cut out your new "Hundreds Counters" to use with your new Thousands' House! They look like this:

Teacher

Please make sure that you take the time to discuss the transition from 100s to 1,000. This concept is difficult for many children. Over the next few days we will be working on understanding how these larger numbers go together. Be looking for and discussing as many patterns in the numbers as you can.

Lets practice writing larger numbers!

For the rest of this lesson, we will be copying numbers from 900–1,000.

Today we will write the numbers 900–925. Discuss any patterns you see.

Numbers for copywork:

900 901 902 903 904

905 906 907 908 909

910 911 912 913 914 915

916 917 918 919 920

921 922 923 924 925

Today we will write the numbers 926–950.
Numbers for copywork:

926 927 928 929 930

931 932 933 934 935

936 937 938 939 940

941 942 943 944 945

946 947 948 949 950

Optional Review: Work with your clock to review what you learned about telling time to the minute.

Name_____

Today we will write the numbers 951–975.
Numbers for copywork:

951 952 953 954 955

956 957 958 959 960

961 962 963 964 965

966 967 968 969 970

971 972 973 974 975

Optional Review: Counting by 2s, 5s, and 10s.

Today we will write the numbers 976–1,000.
Numbers for copywork:

976 977 978 979 980

981 982 983 984 985

986 987 988 989 990

991 992 993 994 995

996 997 998 999 1,000

Optional Review:

We have a triangle with a 6-inch side, a 5-inch side, and a 4-inch side. What is the perimeter?

_____ + _____ + _____ = _____

_____ inches

We have a square with four sides that measure 3 inches each. What is the perimeter?

_____ + _____ = _____

_____ + _____ = _____

_____ + _____ = _____

_____ inches

We have a rectangle with two 7-inch sides and two 2-inch sides. What is the perimeter?

_____ + _____ = _____

_____ + _____ = _____

_____ + _____ = _____

_____ inches

How many bricks are
needed to repair the wall?

_____ bricks

More Work with Subtraction

It was hard to believe! Christmas was only one week away! Yesterday, Mom, Charlie, and Charlotte had spent the entire afternoon listening to Christmas carols and baking Christmas cookies. They had cut out cookies in the shapes of angels, stars, candy canes, snowmen, and holly leaves. What a grand time they had together!

Today, Dad was not working, and he, Charlie, and Charlotte were heading out to chop down their Christmas tree at the tree farm down the road. Mom was staying in the warm house with Ella, due to the freezing temperatures not being favorable for a newborn baby.

As Dad and the children tramped through the fluffy, white snow at the tree farm, they sang carols and laughed, enjoying this time together. Looking closely at each tree, they kept their eyes open for the most magnificent tree for their home.

"Hey, Dad and Charlie!" Charlotte exclaimed, "I found the most beautiful tree ever!"

Charlie, upon inspecting Charlotte's "perfect" tree, had to agree with her! It was beautiful! So tall and majestic-looking, with perfect fullness and shape to its branches, it would look marvelous, all decorated with lights and ornaments, in their living room! Dad nodded his

approval and readied his axe to chop it down. A few minutes later, after dragging the tree to their waiting vehicle and securing it on the roof, they were on their way to show their prize to Mom and Ella!

Arriving home, Dad and Charlie hauled the tree into the living room and put it into the awaiting tree-stand Mom had set up for it. Mom and Charlotte went to the kitchen to make some hot chocolate and arrange some of the beautifully Christmas cookies on a platter for all to enjoy. Sitting in the living room, all four of them agreed this was the most beautiful and most perfect tree yet!

"Hey, Mom," Charlie questioned, "could I please have 5 cookies?"

"No, Charlie," Mother replied, "you may have 2 cookies with your hot chocolate."

"Yes, Mom," Charlie answered, with a smile. "You know, there are eight cookies on the platter. If I eat two and Charlotte eats two, that is subtracting four from the plate. That leaves four for you and Dad. Four plus four is eight, and eight minus four is four."

"Yes, Charlie," Dad added, "and that is what we call a doubles family. Later on, you can make doubles family flashcards if you would like. In the first doubles family we have $1 + 1 = 2$ and $2 - 1 = 1$. In the second, we have $2 + 2 = 4$ and $4 - 2 = 2$, and so on."

Always amazed at the twins' enthusiasm for learning, Dad turned back to the tree, breathing a prayer of thanks to the Lord for sharp minds desiring to learn. He leaned back and enjoyed the sight of his beloved family by the tree.

We have learned a lot about adding and subtracting! In the last few lessons we have learned a lot about adding larger numbers. In this lesson, you will learn about subtracting larger numbers.

Study this example and discuss it with your teacher as he or she reads through the steps.

Some math concepts take a lot of practice, so make sure you take the time to practice and narrate to your teacher what you are learning.

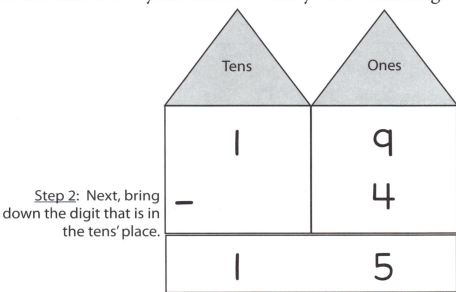

Tens   Ones

1   9
–   4

1   5

Step 1: Line up the digits in the ones' place and the tens' place. In the ones' place, subtract the bottom number from the top number.

Step 2: Next, bring down the digit that is in the tens' place.

Now you try it! Use counting items if you need to!

Tens   Ones
2   5
–   3

Tens   Ones
3   9
–   7

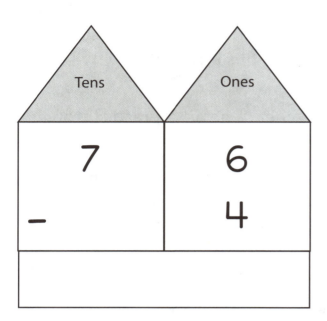

Tens	Ones
7	6
−	4

Tens	Ones
5	3
−	2

Numbers for copywork:

975   976   977   978

979   980   981   982

983   984   985   986

Tens	Ones
8	7
−	2

Tens	Ones
9	2
−	2

Tens	Ones
3	4
−	3

Tens	Ones
4	5
−	4

Numbers for copywork:

987   988   989   990

991   992   993   994

995   996   997   998

999   1,000

Subtraction Practice:

In this exercise, we are going to go a little further in learning to subtract larger numbers. In the last two exercises you have practiced subtracting one-digit numbers from two-digit numbers. Study this example. Follow along carefully as your teacher reads through the steps with you.

<u>First</u>: line up the digits in the ones' place and the tens' place.

<u>Second</u>: subtract the digits in the ones' place first.

<u>Third</u>: subtract the digits in the tens' place.

<u>Last</u>: look at your answer. Does it make sense?

Tens	Ones
3	4
− 2	3
1	1

Now you try it! Talk it through as you work out the following problems. Use counting items if you need to.

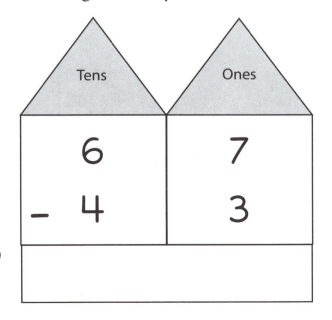

Tens	Ones
6	7
− 4	3

Tens	Ones
3	2
− 1	2

More Practice:

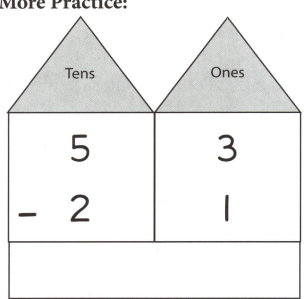

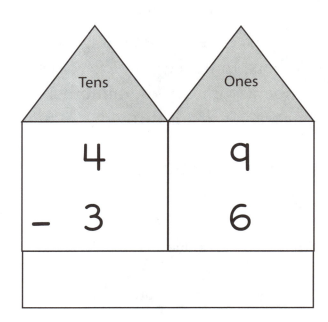

Find the perimeter of these shapes.

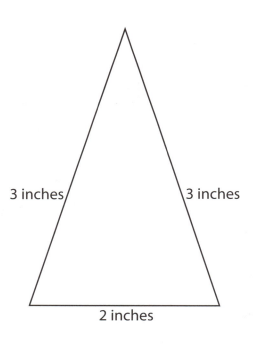

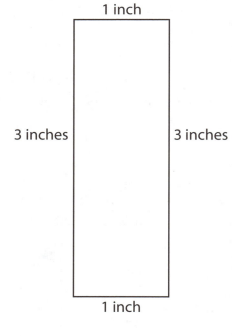

Subtraction Practice:

Now let's practice both! Remember to subtract the ones first.

Tens	Ones
4	6
– 2	1

Tens	Ones
5	4
– 4	3

Tens	Ones
7	9
– 5	6

Tens	Ones
7	5
–	3

Tens	Ones
9	4
–	2

Tens	Ones
8	6
–	5

Draw hands on each clock to show the correct time.

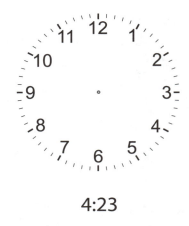

4:23

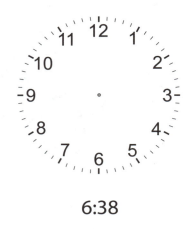

6:38

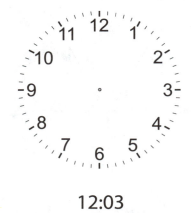

12:03

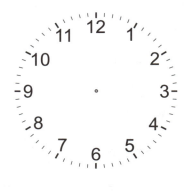

11:08

Subtraction

Have you noticed that when you are subtracting, the larger number is always on top?

Do these hands-on exercises to explore this concept.

☐   Count out 4 items. Can you take 6 away from them? _____

☐   Count out 8 items. Can you take 9 away from them? _____

☐   In the space below, write out both of the above problems. Tell your teacher why they will not work.

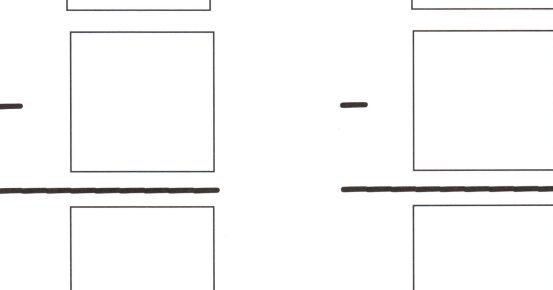

Use these facts for your flashcards:

$2 + 2 = 4$ $7 + 7 = 14$

$4 - 2 = 2$ $14 - 7 = 7$

$3 + 3 = 6$ $8 + 8 = 16$

$6 - 3 = 3$ $16 - 8 = 8$

$4 + 4 = 8$ $9 + 9 = 18$

$8 - 4 = 4$ $18 - 9 = 9$

$5 + 5 = 10$ $10 + 10 = 20$

$10 - 5 = 5$ $20 - 10 = 10$

$6 + 6 = 12$

$12 - 6 = 6$

Introducing Addition with Carrying to the Tens' Place

Christmas Eve Day arrived at last! Grandpa and Grandma were arriving later today, and to help pass the time, Dad offered to teach the twins a new concept in math.

"Yay!" Charlie exclaimed. "What are we learning, Dad?"

"Well, today we will continue to work on adding two numbers and learn what we do when we have more than ten ones in the Ones' House." Grabbing the Larger Addition Mat and placing it in on the table, Dad placed a 1 in the Tens' House, a 6 in the Ones' House and a 5 below it in the Ones' House. "Now, Charlotte, what does 6 + 5 equal?" Dad asked.

"It's 11, Dad. I learned that on my addition flashcards," Charlotte replied.

"Very good, Charlotte, " Dad said.

Charlie, always so eager to grasp new concepts, began, "Dad, 11 is one group of ten and one 'one,' right?"

"Yes, Charlie, you are correct," Dad said as he smiled, "and with that, we need to put the 1 in the Ones' House, and the one group of 10 needs to be added to the Tens' House. Now we

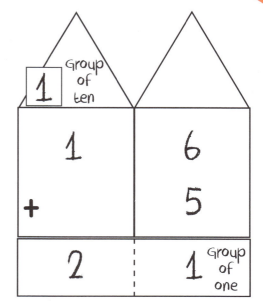

$$16 + 5 = 21$$

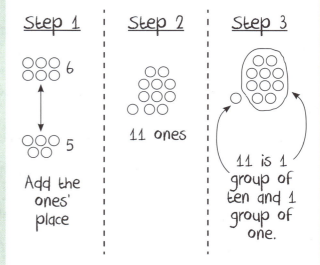

Step 1 — Add the ones' place

Step 2 — 11 ones

Step 3 — 11 is 1 group of ten and 1 group of one.

Step 4

Only 9 ones can live in the Ones' House. We have to move the group of ten to the Tens' House and leave the 1 group of one in the Ones' House.

have 2 groups of tens in the Tens' House," continued Dad, "and so we now know that 16 + 5 = 21. Bringing the one group of ten from the Ones' House to the Tens' House, where it belongs, is called 'carrying.'"

Step 5

When we move the 1 group to the Tens' House, that means we now have 2 groups of ten and 1 group of one, which is 21.

Step 6

We now know that
16 + 5 = 21
or

$$\begin{array}{r} 16 \\ +5 \\ \hline 21 \end{array}$$

"Let's try a few more," Charlotte eagerly suggested.

"Okay," responded Dad, "here we go, Charlotte. How about 22 + 8?"

"Well," Charlotte began, "first we lay it out like this with our Larger Addition Mat."

"Okay, Dad, first we add the Ones' House: 2 + 8 = 10, so we have 1 group of ten, and there are no ones left over. We put a 0 in the Ones' House and carry the one group of ten into the Tens' House. Now we add the Tens' House up. We have 1 + 2, and that is 3 tens, and so 22 + 8 = 30. Is that right, Dad?" Charlotte's bright blue eyes awaited Dad's affirmation, which he gave, "Great job, Charlotte!"

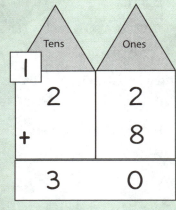

Mom suggested they all play a game while Ella napped. The game proved to be great entertainment, and after it was over, the twins donned their snow apparel and off they went to play in the snow.

Later, after Grandpa and Grandpa arrived, Dad would read the Christmas story by the light of the beautiful Christmas tree, and they would sing "Happy Birthday" to Jesus. After that, they would sing Christmas carols with Grandpa, Grandma, and their parents. Ella would coo softly along with them.

Name_____

Narrate to your teacher the steps of adding with carrying.

Tens	Ones
3	2
+	9

Tens	Ones
6	8
+	4

Tens	Ones
9	4
+	3

Tens	Ones
5	7
+	9

Tens	Ones
4	8
+ 1	2

Tens	Ones
7	6
+ 1	5

Addition Practice.

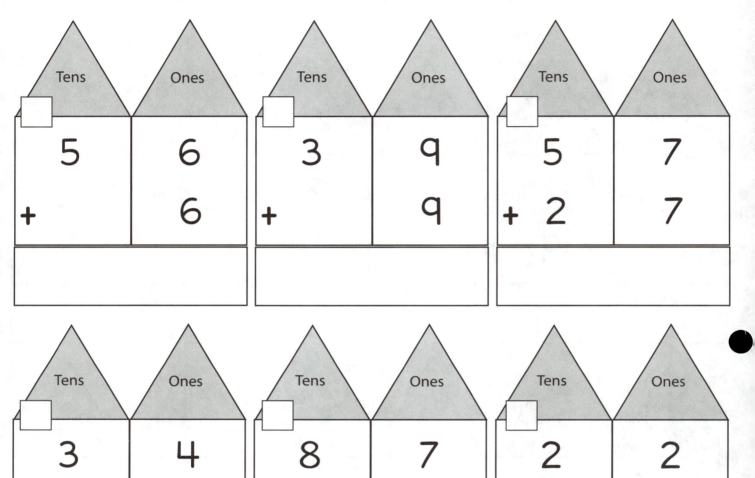

Tens	Ones
5	6
+	6

Tens	Ones
3	9
+	9

Tens	Ones
5	7
+ 2	7

Tens	Ones
3	4
+	8

Tens	Ones
8	7
+	5

Tens	Ones
2	2
+ 6	8

Review addition facts using your flashcards.

Addition Practice.

Tens	Ones
4	9
+	1

Tens	Ones
2	4
+ 1	5

Tens	Ones
9	5
+	1

Tens	Ones
3	5
+ 5	3

Tens	Ones
7	2
+ 1	9

Tens	Ones
5	1
+ 4	6

Solve these addition problems without the "houses" to guide you.

$$
\begin{array}{r} 27 \\ + 54 \\ \hline \end{array}
\qquad
\begin{array}{r} 35 \\ + 16 \\ \hline \end{array}
\qquad
\begin{array}{r} 19 \\ + 74 \\ \hline \end{array}
\qquad
\begin{array}{r} 81 \\ + 27 \\ \hline \end{array}
$$

Complete the Doubles Families Fact Sheet from the back of the book. Make sure it is laminated so you can use it again.

☐ Now it's your turn! Ask your teacher to help you make an equation of your own. Write it in the space and use your counting items to solve. Narrate to your teacher what you are doing as you work through the equation. Tell them if you had to carry or not.

The twins cuddled close to Dad as he read the Christmas story from their Bible storybook. "Long ago, about two thousand years, when King Herod ruled Judea (now part of Israel), God sent the angel, Gabriel, to a young woman who lived in the northern town of Nazareth. The girl's name was Mary, and she was engaged to marry Joseph.

"Gabriel said to Mary, 'Peace be with you! God has blessed you and is pleased with you.' Mary was very surprised by this and wondered what the angel meant. The angel said to her, 'Don't be afraid, God has been very kind to you. You are chosen by God to give birth to a baby boy, and you will call him Jesus. He will be God's own Son and His kingdom will never end.' Mary was very afraid, but she trusted God. 'Let it happen as God says,' she replied to the angel. Gabriel also told Mary that her cousin, Elizabeth, would have a baby boy who God had chosen to prepare the way for Jesus.

"Shortly after this, Mary said goodbye to her family and friends and went to visit her cousin Elizabeth and her husband Zechariah. Elizabeth was very happy to see Mary. She knew that Mary had been chosen by God to be the mother of His Son. An angel had already told Zechariah that Elizabeth's baby would prepare people to welcome Jesus. He was to be called John. Mary stayed with Elizabeth about three months and then returned home to Nazareth.

"Joseph was worried when he found out that Mary was expecting a baby before their marriage had taken place. He wondered if he should put off the wedding altogether. Then an angel appeared to Joseph in a dream and said: 'Don't be afraid to have Mary as your wife.' The angel explained that Mary had been chosen by God to be the mother of his Son and told Joseph that the baby would be named Jesus, which means 'Savior,' because He would save people from their sins. When Joseph woke up, he did what the angel had told him to do and took Mary as his wife.

"At this time, the land where Mary and Joseph lived was part of the Roman Empire. The Roman Emperor Augustus wanted a list of all the people in the empire, to make sure they paid their taxes. He ordered everyone to return to the town where their families originally came from and to enter their names there. Mary and Joseph traveled a long way (about 70 miles) from Nazareth to Bethlehem, because that is where Joseph's family came from. Most people walked, but some people had a donkey to help carry the goods needed for the journey. Joseph and Mary traveled very slowly, because Mary's baby was due to be born soon.

"When they reached Bethlehem, they had problems finding somewhere to stay. So many people had come to register their names that every house was full, and every bed was taken in all of the inns. The only shelter that they could find was a stable with the animals. In this poor place, Jesus, the Son of God, was born. In those days, it was the custom to wrap newborn babies tightly in a long cloth called a 'swaddling cloth.' Jesus' bed was the manger that the animals ate their hay from.

"In the hills and fields outside Bethlehem, shepherds looked after their sheep through the long night. As the new day began, suddenly, an angel appeared before them, and the glory of God shone around them. The shepherds were very, very scared, but the angel said, 'Don't be afraid. I have good news for you and everyone. Today in Bethlehem, a Savior has been born for you. You will find the baby lying in a manger.'

"Then many more angels appeared, lighting up the sky. The shepherds heard them praising God, singing, 'Glory to God in the highest, and peace to everyone on earth.' When the angels had gone, the shepherds said to one another, 'Let's go to Bethlehem to see what has happened.' So the shepherds went to Bethlehem and found Mary and Joseph. The baby Jesus was lying in a manger, as they had been told. When they saw him, they told everyone what the angel had said, and everyone who heard the story was astonished. Then the shepherds returned to their sheep, praising God for sending His Son to be their Savior."

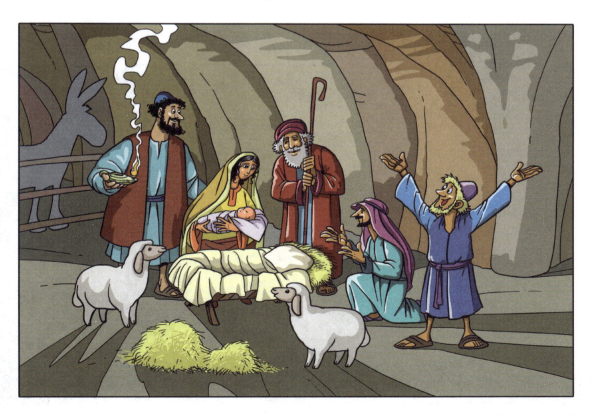

Charlie and Charlotte loved to hear this story every year. Christmas Eve was such a special night. They snuggled close to their dad and gazed at the glittering Christmas tree. They loved the huge evergreen tree, which in their family was a symbol of the eternal life and love of Jesus. The hundreds of lights, glowing through the branches, were a symbol of Jesus being the light of the world. When they decorated the tree together, Mom always told the children that each special ornament that they placed on the tree was a memory of that year of their lives. This year's ornament was in honor of Ella joining their family, a family of five gingerbread people made from modeling clay and painted with each of their names. Jesus had come to earth as a baby, a baby just like Ella. Happy Birthday, Jesus!

Introducing Subtraction with Borrowing from the Tens' Place

Waking up to a beautiful view of fluffy, new snow clothing the evergreens, and a sunny, bright blue sky making the fresh, new snow glisten was just what Charlie and Charlotte needed to jump out of bed and get going with their day! Eagerly entering the kitchen, after seeing to their chores, they nearly knocked their surprised mother down.

"Sorry, Mom," exclaimed Charlie, "I sure didn't mean to do that!"

"It's okay, Charlie," replied Mom, "just remember to slow down a bit."

"Okay, Mom," said Charlie. He continued, "It's SO beautiful outside, isn't it? Did you notice the glistening new snow and the majestic-looking, snow-draped evergreens?"

"Yes, Charlie, I did notice how lovely it is outside," expressed Mom. "Later this morning, we will walk around and take some pictures of the beauty."

"I can hardly wait!" Charlotte chimed in the conversation now. Both children were eagerly anticipating the great enjoyment they were going to have on this glorious January day.

After helping Mom clean up the breakfast dishes and wipe down the counters and table, Charlie and Charlotte patiently began work on their January calendars while Mom fed Ella and then laid her down in her crib. As soon as

Ella was fast asleep for her morning siesta (Mom had explained to them that siesta is the Spanish word for "nap"), Mom told the twins to get ready to go outside with her and take pictures of the beautiful snowy scenery.

With camera in hand, Mom was able to take pictures of the beautiful snow hanging on the evergreen boughs. She also took some photos of different birds visiting the feeders, which the twins were diligently keeping full of food for their feathery friends. Charlotte's favorite picture that Mom took was of a beautiful cardinal on a branch of the snow-clad evergreen. The brilliant red bird shown majestically against the shimmery snowy background.

Sipping hot chocolate with Mom after taking many pictures of the new snow, the twins were eager to learn something new. Dad had taught them about carrying with addition problems before Christmas, and now, they wondered about subtraction.

"Mom," Charlie inquired, "we learned what to do when we are adding and we have more than nine ones in the Ones' House. What happens when we are subtracting, and the number on top in the Ones' House is smaller than the number underneath it in the Ones' House like this?" Charlie demonstrated what he was asking on the blank paper in front of him.

"See, Mom, the 2 is smaller than the 7. We can't take 7 away from 2," Charlie said.

"You're right, Charlie," Mom encouraged, "what we have to do is 'borrow' one ten from the Tens' House, and so in this problem, we take one ten from the 5, thus making only 4 tens left in the Tens' House. Now, Charlotte, how many ones are in that 'ten' that we borrowed?"

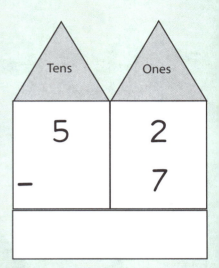

"Ten ones, Mom," replied Charlotte.

"Right, Charlotte," smiled Mom, "and so we take those 10 ones and we add them to the 2 ones on top, making 12 ones, like this." Mom demonstrated on the paper in front of her what she was talking about.

"Now we have 12 ones on top and we subtract 7 from 12, and we get 5. We have 5 ones and 4 tens. So, we say 52 – 7 = 45," further explained Mom.

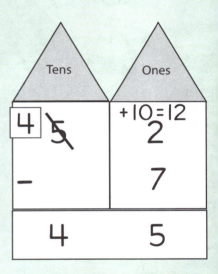

"Now, let's try another one," said Mom, "let's try 81 – 45." The twins took their Larger Subtraction Mat and set up their problem using their manipulatives.

"Okay," Charlotte said, "we can't subtract 5 from 1, so we need to borrow 1 ten from the Tens' House, making the 8 in the Tens' House a 7. Next, we add those 10 ones to the 1 already in the Ones' House, making it an 11. Now we can subtract 11 – 5 in the Ones' House, giving us 6 ones left. And we can subtract 4 from the 7 in the Tens' House, giving us 3 tens left. So we can say 81 – 45 = 36."

"Well done, Charlotte!" exclaimed Mom.

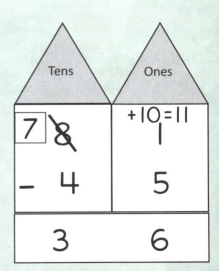

They continued working on subtraction until lunch. After a delicious lunch, Charlie and Charlotte donned their winter clothing once again and raced outdoors to enjoy the beautiful, snowy day.

Teacher

It is extremely important to use manipulatives to work through these problems. This may be a difficult concept to comprehend, so please take the time to practice.

$$
\begin{array}{r}
42 \\
-\ 6 \\
\hline
\end{array}
\qquad
\begin{array}{r}
87 \\
-\ 9 \\
\hline
\end{array}
\qquad
\begin{array}{r}
32 \\
-19 \\
\hline
\end{array}
\qquad
\begin{array}{r}
54 \\
-25 \\
\hline
\end{array}
$$

☐ Practice your doubles with your flashcards.

Subtraction Practice:

More practice on borrowing from the tens' place.

$$
\begin{array}{r} 25 \\ -\ 7 \\ \hline \end{array}
\qquad
\begin{array}{r} 63 \\ -\ 4 \\ \hline \end{array}
\qquad
\begin{array}{r} 82 \\ -75 \\ \hline \end{array}
\qquad
\begin{array}{r} 41 \\ -23 \\ \hline \end{array}
$$

☐   Practice subtraction facts from your flashcards.

Subtraction Practice:

$$\begin{array}{r} 43 \\ -\ 27 \\ \hline \end{array} \qquad \begin{array}{r} 78 \\ -\ 9 \\ \hline \end{array} \qquad \begin{array}{r} 91 \\ -\ 56 \\ \hline \end{array} \qquad \begin{array}{r} 20 \\ -\ 2 \\ \hline \end{array}$$

☐ Practice your subtraction facts using your flashcards.

Subtraction Practice:

$$
\begin{array}{r} 37 \\ -\ 29 \\ \hline \end{array}
\qquad
\begin{array}{r} 54 \\ -\ 29 \\ \hline \end{array}
\qquad
\begin{array}{r} 92 \\ -\ 8 \\ \hline \end{array}
\qquad
\begin{array}{r} 61 \\ -\ 42 \\ \hline \end{array}
$$

☐   Practice using your doubles flashcards.

Review Time!

Now it's your turn! Ask your teacher to help you make up some subtraction equations of your own. Write them in the space below and use your counting items to solve. Narrate to your teacher what you are doing as you work through the equations. Tell them if you had to borrow or not.

Review of Regrouping Concepts

Charlie and Charlotte could hardly believe it! Mom told them that their first year of homeschool was half over this week. They were enjoying it so much. They decided this week they would continue working on subtraction with borrowing and reviewing their addition and subtraction facts. Baby Ella, now three months old and entirely captivated with her older siblings, cooed quietly as she kept her bright blue eyes on them.

We have learned so much in our study! It is important to take time to review and practice all the new concepts we have learned. Throughout the week, work on the next month of your calendar.

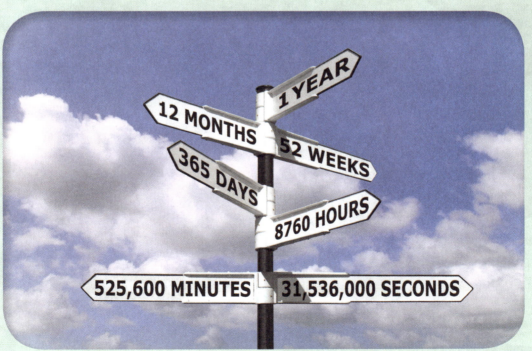

Review Time!

What are the shapes we have learned so far?

Draw a circle:

Draw a square:

Draw a rectangle:

Draw a triangle:

Draw an oval:

Divide each of the following shapes into the shown fractions. Narrate to your teacher what makes a true fraction.

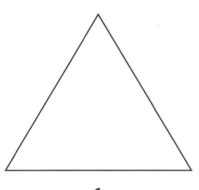

$\frac{1}{2}$

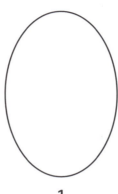

$\frac{1}{2}$

$\frac{1}{4}$

$\frac{1}{4}$

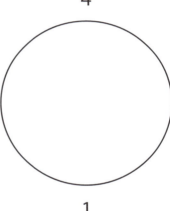

$\frac{1}{2}$

Color each $\frac{1}{4}$ red and each $\frac{1}{2}$ blue.

Review Time! Draw hands on each clock to show the correct time.

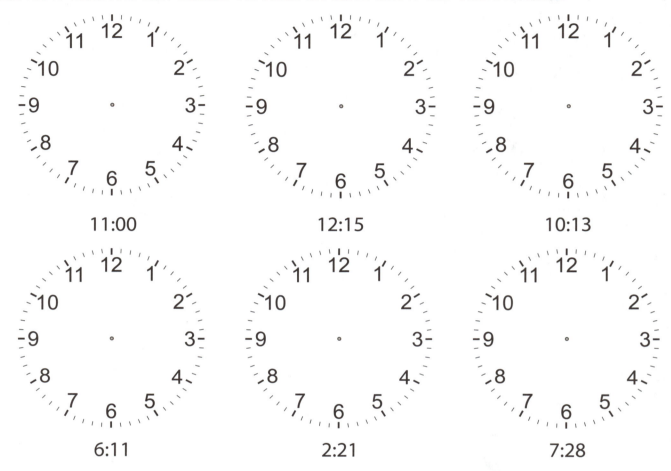

11:00   12:15   10:13

6:11   2:21   7:28

Count these sets of coins and write the correct amount.

_____ ¢

_____ ¢

_____ ¢

_____ ¢

Review Time!

In the spaces below, write the numbers as you count by:

2s from 0–20

5s from 0–50

10s from 0–100

☐   Use your flashcards to practice any facts that you may still be working on.

Review Time!

Solve these word problems.

Word Problem 1:

Charlotte and Charlie have fun playing with Ella. The baby has giggled 3 times at Charlie and 8 times at Charlotte. How many times all together have the twins gotten their baby sister to giggle?

Word Problem 2:

Charlotte and Grandma made small, fleece blankets for the children in the orphanage in Peru. Grandma tied the ties on 8 fleece blankets, and Charlotte tied 4 blankets. How many blankets did they make all together?

Word Problem 3:

Charlie and Dad worked together to ready the sheeps' pen for winter. They nailed 10 boards on the north side of the pen and 5 boards on the south side. How many more boards did they nail on the north side?

Word Problem 4:

The twins loved their new schoolroom. They decorated the walls with pictures that they had drawn. On the left wall they hung 15 pictures, and on the right wall they hung 7 pictures. How many more pictures were on the left wall than the right?

Word Problem 5:

If the twins combine all of their building blocks, they can build a large castle in their schoolroom. Mom said that they could build a castle together after they were finished with their thank you notes to Grandma and Grandpa. Charlie has 9 tubs of blocks, and Charlotte has 7 tubs of blocks. How many tubs do they have all together?

Name_____

Review Time!

Dear Grandma and Grandpa,

   Thank you so much for the wonderful gifts that you sent us! We love the new jump ropes and the board game. We have been having so much fun playing with Ella! She is getting so big and loves to giggle at us when we play peek-a-boo with her. We have been working hard in school, too! Here are some of the exciting new concepts we have learned in math.

   We learned to solve these REALLY big addition and subtraction problems:

$$\begin{array}{r} 76 \\ -58 \\ \hline \end{array} \qquad \begin{array}{r} 42 \\ +9 \\ \hline \end{array}$$

We have also been practicing measuring things around our house.

Here is a line that is 4 inches long:

Here is a square that has 1-inch sides. The perimeter of the square is:

_____ + _____ = _____

_____ + _____ = _____

_____ + _____ = _____

_____ inches

We love you!

Charlie, Charlotte, and our friend, _____

Understanding Dollars and Cents — Writing Money Terms

Charlie and Charlotte were ready for another trip to the bank. They had been saving their pennies, nickels, dimes, quarters, and even a couple of dollar bills for Hairo and Natalia, their friends from the orphanage in South America. Today, Mom had promised to help them count out their coins and bills and then take them to the bank. Eagerly and diligently finishing their other schoolwork, the twins were now ready to count their change.

Mom, having just put Ella down for her morning siesta, joined Charlie and Charlotte at the table. Dumping the coins on the table, the twins began separating the coins. Mom grabbed a piece of paper and a pencil from the drawer and began showing the kids another way to write amounts for pennies, nickels, dimes, and quarters. She explained that for amounts up to 99¢, you could just add the (¢) sign to the right side of the number. She further demonstrated writing monetary values by using a decimal point, which looked just like a period, with a dollar sign ($) in front of it.

"See, Charlie and Charlotte, you can write the value of a penny as 1¢ or as $.01. They both are said as 'one cent.' A nickel's value can be written as 5¢ or as $ .05 and said as 'five cents.' The reason we need the '0' in the number after the decimal point is to be a 'place holder.' We always need two numbers to the right of the decimal point when writing any monetary values. With a dime, we write the value as 10¢ or as $ .10 and say it as 'ten cents.' Instead of writing 100¢, we write the value for one dollar as $1.00. The two places to the right of the decimal point show how many 'cents' we have; in this case, we have one dollar and zero cents. Let's practice writing money values together."

Trace the dollar signs:

$ $ $ $ $ $ $

Write each money value showing both ways of writing it. The first one is done for you.

4 cents	4¢	$ .04
8 cents	_____	_____
35 cents	_____	_____
100 cents	_____	_____
67 cents	_____	_____
55 cents	_____	_____
1 cent	_____	_____
3 cents	_____	_____

_____ ¢

$._____

_____ ¢

$._____

More practice!

Using your money, count out the following amounts. In the space next to each, write the value both ways. Narrate to your teacher what you are doing.

☐   8 dimes   _____   _____

☐   7 pennies   _____   _____

☐   9 nickels   _____   _____

☐   4 dimes   _____   _____

☐   2 dimes   _____   _____

☐   10 dimes   _____   _____

☐   6 nickels   _____   _____

☐   3 pennies   _____   _____

☐   5 pennies   _____   _____

Solve these word problems. Remember the steps.

Word Problem 1:

If Charlie has 6 dimes and Charlotte has 4 dimes, what is the total value of their money all together? Write it both ways.

Word Problem 2:

Mom and Dad wanted to donate some money to send to the children in Peru, also. Mom had 7 nickels and Dad had 10 nickels to give. What is the value of their money all together? Write it both ways.

After practicing writing money values using the decimal point, Mom and the twins began counting their coins.

"Hey!" Charlotte enthusiastically exclaimed, "ten dimes equal one dollar, but it takes twenty nickels to equal one dollar. It takes one hundred pennies to equal one dollar."

"You're absolutely right, Charlotte," encouraged Mom, "and I see you have four quarters in one of your piles. Four quarters also equal one dollar. Two quarters are equal to 50¢, which is half of a dollar." With Mom's suggestion, the twins decided to make a Money Facts Sheet, showing different ways to make one dollar.

I dollar

I quarter

Use your money to count and fill in the money chart on the following page.
Optional: Draw pictures of the coins that you counted.

Money Facts Sheet.

What Makes a Dollar?

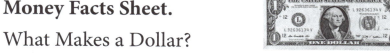

(You don't have to draw this!)

_____ pennies

_____ nickels

_____ dimes

_____ quarters

Charlie had counted out all of his coins for his friend Hairo. Help Charlie make a list of the amounts of money, for each kind of coin, he had. Write it both ways.

_____ ¢

$. _____

_____ ¢

$. _____

_____ ¢

$. _____

_____ ¢

$. _____

_____ ¢

$ ___ . _____

Charlie was so excited to know how much this equaled in all. Mom showed him how to add it all up. He then proudly wrote the amount on his paper, gathered all the coins and the dollar bill, and put them in a baggie, zipped the baggie shut, and readied himself for town. Mom helped Charlotte total her money as well, and right after lunch they were off to the bank, where the friendly bank teller assisted them once again in counting their money.

Charlie and Charlotte are making flashcards to learn these new money concepts. Take time to start working on your money concept flashcards, also.

Using blank index cards, create money concept flashcards by drawing pictures of the coins and the dollar bill and writing the following:

- 1 penny = 1¢
- 1 nickel = $0.05 (or 5¢)
- 1 dime = $0.10 (or 10¢)
- 1 quarter = $0.25 (or 25¢)
- 1 dollar = $1.00 (or 100¢)

Review Time!

Check off each one as you complete it.

☐   Count out 1 dollar in dimes. How many dimes? _____

☐   Count out 1 dollar in nickels. How many nickels? _____

☐   Count out 50¢ in pennies. How many pennies? _____

☐   With your teacher's help, count out 50¢ in quarters. How many quarters? _____

☐   **Bonus:** Try to count out 33¢ using a combination of dimes and pennies. How many dimes? _____ How many pennies? _____

☐   Finish your money concept flashcards and review.

Review — Money

Skipping into the post office the next day, with dazzling smiles on their adorable faces, Charlie and Charlotte grasped their envelopes securely and brought them to the postmaster.

"We would like to send these letters to Peru. That is in South America by the Andes Mountains and the Amazon Rainforest," Charlie vivaciously explained to the rather amused postmaster. Mom had just shared this information with the twins a few days before, and true to his nature, Charlie just had to share it with someone else.

"Well, okee dokee, we will get them delivered to Peru for you,"

replied the kind postmaster as he weighed and stamped the envelopes.

"Thank you," both children graciously responded at once.

Mom paid the postage, picked up Ella, who was strapped securely in her car seat, and the four exited the post office.

Arriving home, Charlie and Charlotte each grabbed a book from the book basket in the family room and quietly read for the next half hour, while Mom fed Ella and then prepared lunch for them. It had been so fun and rewarding to send Hairo and Natalia letters.

Review Time!

Using your money, count out these amounts to your teacher.

- ☐ $ .05 in pennies
- ☐ $ .15 in nickels
- ☐ $ .70 in dimes
- ☐ $ 1.00 in nickels
- ☐ $ .16 in pennies
- ☐ $ .40 in dimes
- ☐ $ .50 in quarters
- ☐ **Bonus:** Try counting out $ 1.00 using a combination of dimes and nickels. How many dimes did you use? _____ How many nickels did you use? _____

More Review!

Practice doing these subtraction problems.

$$
\begin{array}{r} 25 \\ -18 \\ \hline \end{array}
\qquad
\begin{array}{r} 67 \\ -34 \\ \hline \end{array}
\qquad
\begin{array}{r} 86 \\ -29 \\ \hline \end{array}
\qquad
\begin{array}{r} 51 \\ -47 \\ \hline \end{array}
$$

Name the Number.

In the following numbers, tell what place the underlined number is in. The first one has been done for you.

645   tens' place

1,323   _____

798   _____

42   _____

2,222   _____

3,102   _____

4,678   _____

9,999   _____

Solve the following addition problems.

$$
\begin{array}{r}
67 \\
+\ 38 \\
\hline
\end{array}
\qquad
\begin{array}{r}
45 \\
+\ 29 \\
\hline
\end{array}
$$

Review Time!

Solve the following word problems.

Word Problem 1:

Charlie was busy working in the garage. He was sawing a board in the shape of a rectangle. He needed two sides to be 4 inches long and two sides to be 6 inches long. Draw out the rectangle, labeling the sides, and then figure out the perimeter of the rectangle.

Word Problem 2:

Charlotte and her grandma were cutting out more fleece blankets for the children at the orphanage in Peru. They needed each side to be 5 feet long. Draw a picture of the square-shaped blanket, label the sides, and solve for the perimeter.

Review Time! Count the following money and write the value on the line. The first one has been done for you.

| 10¢ | 20¢ | 30¢ | 40¢ | 50¢ | 60¢ | 70¢ |

90¢

75¢ 80¢ 85¢ 90¢

_____

_____

_____

Practice your facts with My Addition Mat.

Review Time!

Draw lines for the following measurements.

4 inches

5 inches

1 inch

3 inches

2 inches

Fill in the clock faces to match the times.

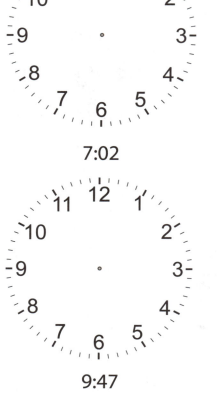
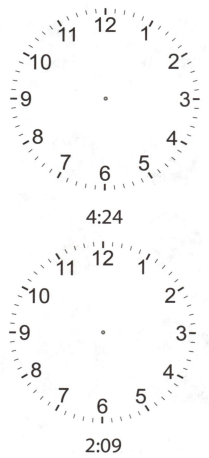

6:30   7:02   4:24

12:01   9:47   2:09

Introducing Thermometers and Other Gauges

Cuddled up next to Dad and Mom on the couch on this freezing, blowing, snowy day, Charlie and Charlotte were eager to know more about blizzards.

"What exactly is a blizzard, Dad?" asked Charlotte, knowing this was the reason Dad got to be home with them today.

"Well, it is a severe winter storm, which can last for a few hours or more. In a blizzard, the temperatures fall and are very low, and winds blow 35 miles per hour or more. With snow falling and winds blowing, we cannot see much except white, swirling snow. It can be very dangerous to be outside during a blizzard due to the freezing temperatures and reduced visibilities. You can get frostbite from the freezing temperatures, and you can lose your way with the reduced visibility."

"Wow!" Charlie exclaimed. "I sure am glad we have a warm, cozy house!"

"We most definitely can be thankful for that!" agreed Mom, with a smile.

Rising from the couch, Dad strolled over to the window for a look at the thermometer. Charlie popped up off the couch and joined Dad at the frosty window. Charlotte and Mom decided to take a peek outside, too.

"Wow!" exclaimed Charlie. "The thermometer says it is way below zero, Dad!"

"Yes, it does," agreed Dad. "Temperature means how hot something is. It is measured using a thermometer. It is measured in degrees Fahrenheit (°F) or degrees Centigrade (°C). For instance, normal room temperature is 20°C, which is 68°F. Normal body temperature is 37°C, which is 98.6°F. Water freezes at 0°C, which is 32°F, and water boils at 100°C, which is 212°F.

Keeping a weather and temperature journal can be a very interesting thing to do. You can record the daily temperature, you can write down what the sky looks like and what kinds of clouds you see, if any, and what is happening in nature all around you."

"How do you read a thermometer, Dad?" questioned Charlotte.

"Well, there is liquid in a narrow tube in the thermometer. As the liquid warms up, it gets bigger and fills more of the tube, causing the red or black line, which is the liquid inside the thermometer, to raise and lower. Heat generally causes liquids to expand, or get bigger, and that is why the liquid rises when temperatures go up."

While the wind howled and the snow continued to blow ferociously, Dad helped Charlie and Charlotte take their own body temperatures, and he assisted them in boiling water and taking the temperature. Learning how to take temperature and read a thermometer was lots of fun!

Dad further explained to the twins about the differences in temperature in different areas of the world. The twins wondered what the temperature was like in Peru, South America. Dad responded by telling them that Peru has mountainous areas, which can be very cold and snowy on the peaks (which are the pointy tops of mountains), but lower down are great for growing crops, with milder temperatures on the lower slopes. Also, Peru has hot, desert areas which are dry and very, very warm. In addition, Dad pointed out that Peru borders the Amazon Rainforest, which is the biggest rainforest in the world and has very warm temperatures all year round. After discussing weather and temperature in South America, Dad suggested they read an entertaining story about some of the animals in the Amazon. Both kids readily and excitedly agreed. The three cuddled up and read about a place thousands of miles away which is hot and humid, while the freezing, icy winds continued to howl outside their home.

Attention: You will need a candy thermometer and simple ingredients for Exercise 4 of this lesson.

Study the thermometer below and answer these questions. Talk through this with your teacher.

1. What temperature does the thermometer show? _____

2. Do the numbers start smaller and get bigger as you go up the thermometer? _____

3. Study the small lines between the numbers. How many are there? _____

4. When we read the temperature, what do we count by? What does each small line stand for? _____

5. The numbers on the thermometer are going up as if counting by _____.

°F

120
100
80
60
40
20
0

Important note:

At the end of this lesson, there is a page with 7 thermometers for you to fill in daily over the next week.

We will be using these thermometers in a coming lesson for a graphing project.

Please make sure that you check the temperature every day and fill in the correct temperature on that day's thermometer.

Over the next two days, you will be working through some hands-on projects that explore the concept of temperature and reading thermometers. Do one section each day.

IMPORTANT: TEACHER MUST HELP WITH THIS!

Note: it will take at least several minutes in each location to get an accurate reading.

Use your thermometer to measure the temperature in these locations:

☐ If you have a basement, cellar, or three-season porch.

Temperature _____ °F

☐ Inside the refrigerator. Temperature _____ °F

☐ Inside your bedroom. Temperature _____ °F

☐ Next to a turned-on lamp. Temperature _____ °F

☐ Near a closed window. Temperature _____ °F

☐ Inside the freezer. Temperature _____ °F

☐ If you have a multi-level home, take the temperature on each level and note any differences in temperature. _____ °F, _____ °F

IMPORTANT: TEACHER MUST HELP WITH THIS!

Use your thermometer to measure the temperature in these items:

☐ If you have snow, place your thermometer in the snowbank. If you do not have snow available, put ice in a drinking glass, add water, and record the temperature. Temperature _____ °F

☐ **HAVE YOUR TEACHER DO ALL OF THE FOLLOWING:** In a saucepan, boil some water on the stove. After boiling, remove pan from stove top. Place your thermometer carefully into the boiling water for a few minutes. Remove the thermometer from the water and read temperature. Temperature _____ °F

☐ Make your own practice thermometer. Follow these directions:

1. Gather white card stock (8.5 x 11 is a good size), a pencil, markers, a ruler, a hole punch, red yarn, scissors, a square of black construction paper (1-inch square), a stapler, and a small amount of poster putty.

2. Fold card stock in half lengthwise. Cut in half on the fold.

3. Ask your teacher to measure and lightly write (with the pencil) the lines and numbers on your thermometer. Use the thermometer in this lesson (Exercise 1) as a guide.

4. Now go over the pencil lines with your black marker.

5. Use the hole punch to make a hole at the bottom of your thermometer.

6. Cut a length of red yarn a few inches longer than your thermometer.

7. Tie a big enough knot at the end of your yarn to keep it from pulling through the hole in the card stock. Thread the yarn through the hole before doing the next step.

8. Fold the 1-inch square of black construction paper in half. Place it over the end of the yarn opposite the knot. Staple the square firmly onto the yarn, catching all the layers of paper and yarn together.

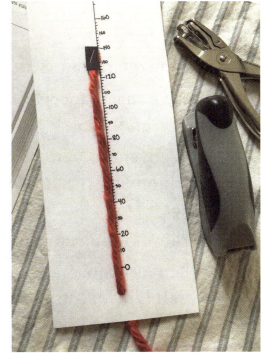

9. Place a small amount of the poster putty on the folded square.

10. Now you can use your thermometer to practice reading temperatures by pulling the yarn up and sticking the black square at the correct temperature.

We have a very exciting project today! We will be making salt water taffy using a candy thermometer.

IMPORTANT: TEACHER MUST HELP WITH THIS!

Salt Water Taffy

1 cup sugar

$\frac{3}{4}$ cup light corn syrup

$\frac{2}{3}$ cup water

1 tablespoon cornstarch

2 tablespoons butter or margarine

1 teaspoon salt

2 teaspoons vanilla

Directions:

1. Butter square pan, 8 x 8 x 2 inches

2. In two-quart saucepan, combine sugar, corn syrup, water, cornstarch, butter, and salt.

3. Cook over medium heat, stirring constantly, to 256 degrees F on candy thermometer (or until small amount of mixture dropped into very cold water forms a hard ball).

4. Remove from heat; stir in vanilla. Pour into pan.

5. When just cool enough to handle, pull taffy until satiny, light in color, and stiff. If taffy becomes sticky, butter hands lightly.

6. With scissors, cut strips into one-inch pieces.

7. Wrap pieces individually in wax paper. Candy must be wrapped to hold shape. Makes about 1 pound.

Review Time!

Dear Hairo and Natalia,

We are so excited to write to you again, so we can show you what we have learned! Dad is teaching us all sorts of wonderful things about where you live. We have also been learning about temperatures and thermometers. We have been doing many different projects exploring these concepts.

One of our favorite projects was making salt water taffy. It is so yummy! We wish we could send you some, but Mom said that it would be stale by the time it would get to you.

We want to show you what a thermometer looks like. (Help the twins show their friends what a thermometer looks like by drawing one in the space below.)

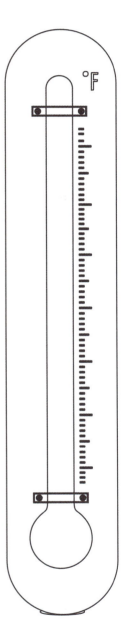

Write back soon and tell us about the temperatures you are having down there in South America. We love to get letters from you!

Love,

Charlie, Charlotte, and our friend, _____

Sunday

_____ °F

Monday

_____ °F

Tuesday

_____ °F

Wednesday

_____ °F

Thursday

_____ °F

Friday

_____ °F

Saturday

_____ °F

Keep these pages for another project in a coming lesson.

Reading Bar Graphs and Line Graphs

After learning all about temperature and thermometers, Charlie and Charlotte had been keeping track of daily temperatures. Being February in the Midwest, they were observing quite a range of temperatures in their weather journals. Just this morning, Mom had shown the twins the difference between a line graph and a bar graph. Mom provided them with some graph paper, and now they were busily trying to record the temperatures, for this week in February, on a line graph like this:

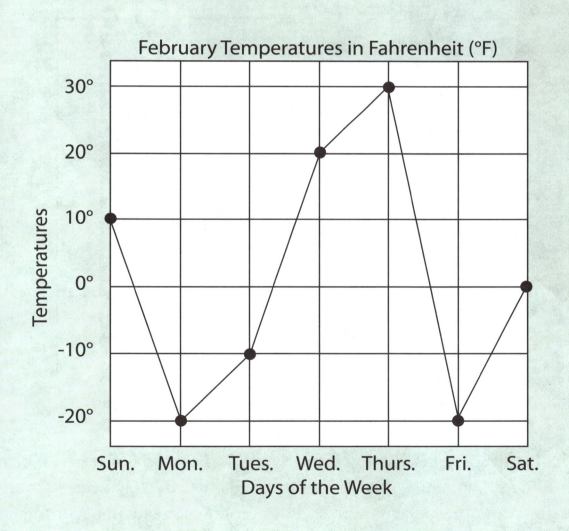

Charlotte also had been keeping track of how many various kinds of birds were coming to their feeders. Mom had provided her with a birding field guide, and now she was busy designing a bar graph with her info, like this:

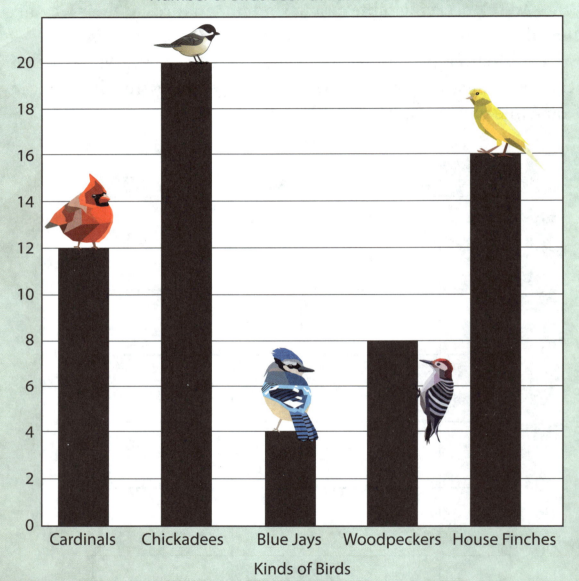

Number of Birds Seen at Feeders in a Week

Kinds of Birds

Charlotte had read some fascinating information in her bird guide about black-capped chickadees. Evidently, these cute little birds that she had seen so many of over the past week, had to eat their weight in food each day in order to keep their body temperature of 108°F steady. The cardinal still was the prettiest bird she observed, in her opinion.

Using graphs helps us organize information in a clear, concise way. The first graph in this lesson (which graphed temperatures) is called a line graph. For instance, on the line graph, we see the differences in temperatures during one week in February. The dots tell us what the actual temperature, taken on a certain day, is. For example, if we wanted to know what the temperature was on Wednesday, we first of all go to the column marked "Wed." for Wednesday. From there, we follow the "Wed." line up to the dot. Next, we follow the line to the left until we see the temperature, which, in this case, is 20°F.

Using the temperature line graph on page 205, talk through the following questions with your teacher. Write the answers on the lines.

☐   What was the warmest day in the week? _____

☐   What was the temperature on Monday? _____ °F

☐   What was the coldest day in the week? _____

☐   What was the temperature on Saturday? _____ °F

☐   What two days had a temperature of -20°F? _____ and _____.

☐   **Bonus!** What was the difference in temperature between Wednesday and Thursday? (Tip: "difference" always means "subtract") _____°F.

☐   Calendar reminder! Make sure your calendar is current.

Bar graphs are another way to organize information. Using Charlotte's bird bar graph on page 206, answer the following questions.

- ☐   What bird did Charlotte see the most of at the feeders? _____
- ☐   How many bluejays did Charlotte see? _____
- ☐   What kind of bird did Charlotte see 12 of at the feeders? _____
- ☐   How many house finches came to the feeders? _____
- ☐   **Bonus!** How many more chickadees came than bluejays? (Tip: "how many more" means "subtract.") _____

Fill in the thermometers to show the correct temperatures.

60 °F   110 °F   32 °F

Line Graph Practice.

Using the temperatures that you recorded in Lesson 21, make a line graph below. Have your teacher help you. Use a ruler to connect your dots, day to day, after you have graphed your information. You will need to write in the temperatures on the left-hand side of the graph. Also, write a title for your graph on the line provided at the top.

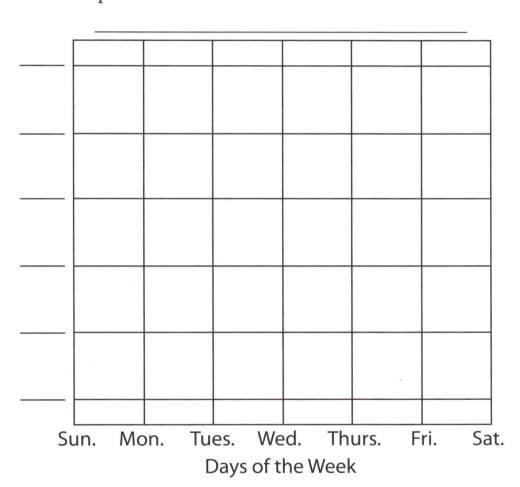

Days of the Week

Explain to your teacher what you did. Make up questions to quiz your teacher!

Graphs:

Study the bar graph and answer the questions.

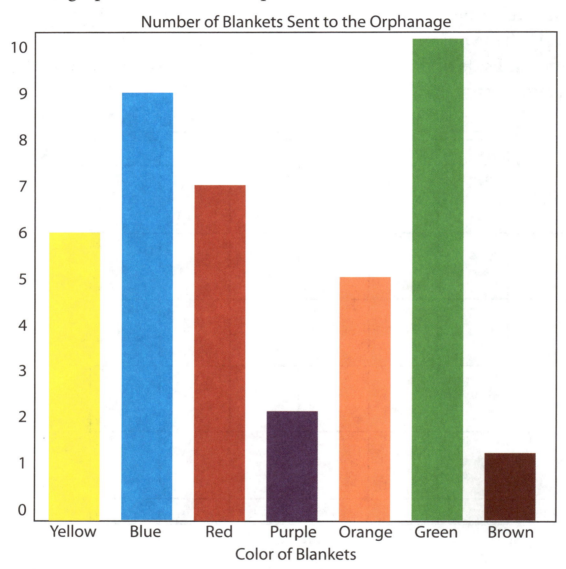

Number of Blankets Sent to the Orphanage

Color of Blankets

☐   What color of blankets did they send the most of to the orphanage?

   _____

☐   How many orange blankets did they send? _____

☐   What is the title of this bar graph? _____

   _____

Write a number sentence.

☐   How many more yellow blankets did they send than purple blankets? ____

☐   How many red and blue blankets did they send all together? _____

☐   What color did they send 9 of? _____

☐   How many brown blankets did they send? _____

☐   What color of blankets did they send the least of to the orphanage?

     _____

☐   **Big Bonus!!** How many blankets did they send in all? (Tip: "in all" means "add.")

Bar Graphs.

Using your temperature readings from Lesson 21, make a bar graph of your own.

Write the temperatures down the left side (like you did for the line graph) and the days of the week along the bottom. Draw bars to show the temperature each day. Title your graph.

_____

More on Measurement — Pounds and Ounces

Going to the clinic with Mom for Ella's checkup was a delight for Charlotte! Charlie had stayed home to help Dad with some building projects in the garage, and she had been able to come with Mom. She was SO excited! She remembered when Ella was a newborn, and she had come to the hospital to meet her new baby sister and to see Mom and Dad. She had been so excited then, too.

As the nurse led them to the exam room, she stopped first at a little padded table with edges, where she weighed Ella.

"Fourteen pounds, three ounces!" the nurse announced. Next, she laid Ella down with her head at one end of the table and measured how tall she was.

"Thirty-one inches long," added the nurse. After measuring around Ella's head to make sure everything was growing as it should, the nurse continued leading them down the hall to the exam room. Mom answered several questions about Ella's development while Charlotte entertained Ella with the toys from the diaper bag.

As they waited for the doctor to arrive, Mom explained to Charlotte that 16 ounces is the same as one pound.

She further explained that half a pound always equals 8 ounces.

"When we arrive home, Charlotte," said Mom, "I have a small scale which you and Charlie can weigh things on. After that, we will begin making some measurement flashcards, okay?"

"That would be great, Mom," responded Charlotte.

The rest of Ella's appointment went well. The doctor said she was growing well and she was happy to hear what a contented baby she was.

True to her word, Mom found the scale when they arrived home. Explaining to Charlie that 16 ounces, which is abbreviated "16 oz," is equal to 1 pound, which is abbreviated "1 lb," Mom handed each twin a sheet of paper and a pencil to record their findings. Charlie and Charlotte found many things to weigh and were really enjoying sketching the objects on their papers and recording the objects' weights next to the drawings. This kept them busy for quite awhile.

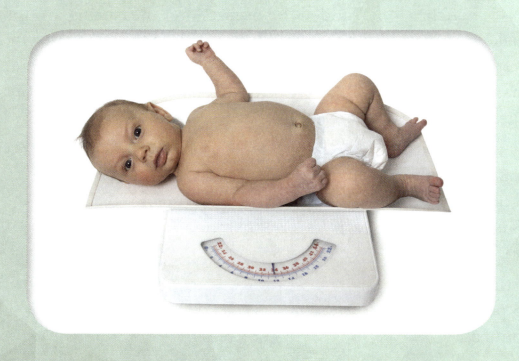

You are also going to create flashcards to review weights. Spend some time today working on this project. You will want to decorate them with pictures to help you remember what each weight stands for. For example, you could draw a picture of a loaf of bread because a loaf of bread is usually about a pound.

Look at the pictures below. Decide if you would use ounces or pounds to measure their weight. Under each picture write either oz. or lbs.

_____   _____   _____

_____   _____   _____

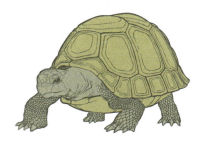      

_____   _____   _____

Time to Explore!

Today you will be doing some exploring! Below is a scavenger hunt list. Write the amount of ounces each item weighs. At the end of the list are five places to write some things you find on your own.

- ☐ tube of toothpaste _____ oz.

- ☐ can of soup _____ oz.

- ☐ small bag of frozen veggies _____ oz.

- ☐ gallon of milk or juice _____ oz.

- ☐ shampoo bottle _____ oz.

- ☐ loaf of bread _____ oz.

- ☐ stick of butter _____ oz.

- ☐ _____ oz. What is it? _____

- ☐ _____ oz. What is it? _____

- ☐ _____ oz. What is it? _____

- ☐ _____ oz. What is it? _____

For copywork:

16 ounces = 1 pound

What are the abbreviations?

ounces _____   pound _____

More exploring!

Today's scavenger hunt list shows items that are weighed using pounds. Write how many pounds each one weighs. At the end of the list are five places to write some things you find on your own.

☐   bag of sugar _____ lbs.

☐   bag of flour _____ lbs.

☐   your younger sibling _____ lbs.

☐   yourself _____ lbs.

☐   one of your parents _____ lbs.

☐   your math book _____ lbs.

☐   _____ lbs. What is it? _____

☐   _____ lbs. What is it? _____

☐   _____ lbs. What is it? _____

☐   _____ lbs. What is it? _____

☐   _____ lbs. What is it? _____

Ask your parent how much you weighed as a newborn. _____

If you have siblings, how much did they weigh? Write their weights in the space below. (Make sure you write their names next to the weight.)

_____   _____ lb. _____ oz.

_____   _____ lb. _____ oz.

_____   _____ lb. _____ oz.

_____   _____ lb. _____ oz.

Use the weights you discovered in Exercise 2 to fill in the bars in this bar graph. Title your graph. Explain to your teacher what you are doing.

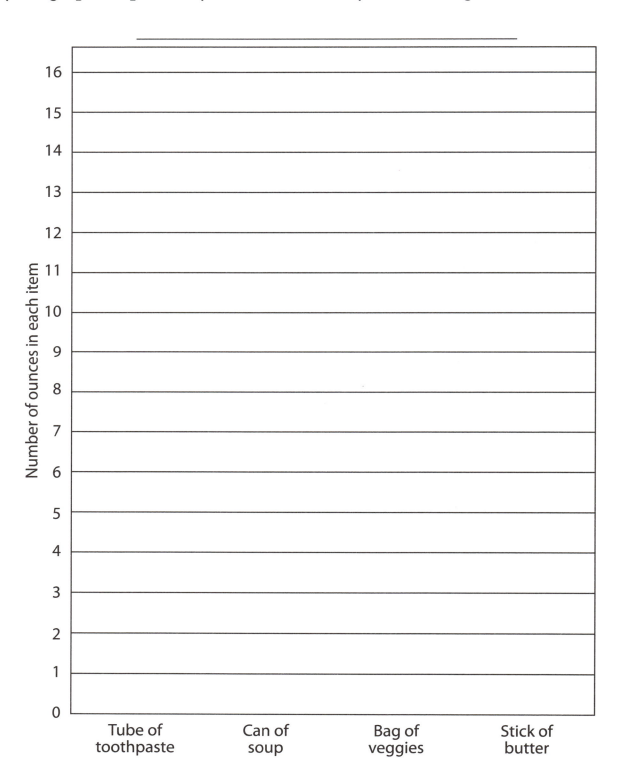

Review Time!

Study the line graph showing the weights in pounds. Answer the questions.

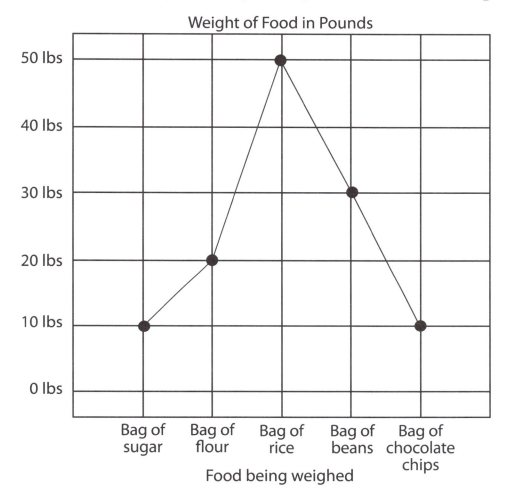

How much does the bag of rice weigh? _____ lbs.

How much does the bag of sugar weigh? _____ lbs.

How much does the bag of flour weigh? _____ lbs.

How much does the bag of beans weigh? _____ lbs.

How much does the bag of chocolate chips weigh? _____ lbs.

What is the temperature? Write the temperature under each thermometer.

_____ °F   _____ °F   _____ °F

More Measurement Concepts — Gallons, Quarts, Pints, Cups

Nothing thrilled the twins more these days than receiving mail from Hairo and Natalia. The letters their Peruvian friends wrote needed to be translated by someone who could speak both English and Spanish so Charlie and Charlotte could read them. Mom was teaching the children how to count in Spanish (uno, dos, tres, cuatro, cinco, seis, siete, ocho, nueve, diez), the Spanish alphabet, and how to sing "Jesus Loves Me" in Spanish, but they were far from being able to interpret Hairo and Natalia's letters in Spanish without help from a translator. Thankfully, there was such a person at the orphanage who could read, write, and speak both Spanish and English. The translator wrote the letters in English before sending them off to the very eager twins in the United States. Today, the letters had contained a couple of recipes for Charlie and Charlotte to make with Mom. They could hardly wait to begin cooking these South American specialities. The first one was "Papas a la Huancaina" (Potatoes with Cheese). The recipe read as follows:

Papas a la Huancaina (Potatoes with Cheese)

8 potatoes, peeled and cubed

water

$1\frac{1}{2}$ cups heavy cream

$\frac{1}{2}$ tsp. turmeric

3 cups Monterey Jack cheese

1. Boil the potatoes, covered, until tender. Drain and set aside.

2. In a small saucepan, heat cream over low heat. Do not allow it to boil. Stir in cheese and turmeric. Continue to stir until cheese is melted. Add potatoes, cooking until potatoes are heated through. Serve warm or cold.

The other recipe was called "Alfajores" (or Caramel-filled Cookies). It read as follows:

Alfajores (Caramel-filled Cookies)

2 cups cornstarch	2 eggs
1 cup flour	1 tsp. vanilla
1 cup sugar	3 tbsp. milk
$\frac{1}{2}$ tsp. baking powder	1 can (13.4 oz.) Dulce de Leche*
$\frac{3}{4}$ cup butter, room temp.	Powdered sugar

1. Preheat oven to 300°F. Combine dry ingredients in a large bowl. Cut in butter and stir until mixture resembles coarse crumbs. Add eggs, vanilla, and milk. Knead until smooth. Let dough rest for 20 minutes.

2. Roll dough out at about $\frac{1}{4}$ inch thickness. Cut out cookies with a cookie cutter. Bake for 20 minutes or until cookies begin to brown. Remove from oven and cool.

3. Spread dulce de leche on one side of the cookie and top with another cookie. Roll cookie sandwich in powdered sugar. Repeat with remaining cookies. Serve.

Dulce de Leche*

1 can sweetened condensed milk

1. Remove label from can. Pierce the top, using a can opener, with two holes.

2. Place in a pot, pierced end up, and fill pot with water about $\frac{1}{4}$ inch from the top of the can.

3. Bring to a boil. Reduce heat and simmer, uncovered, for 3 hours. You may need to add more water as the water evaporates.

4. Remove from water and cool.

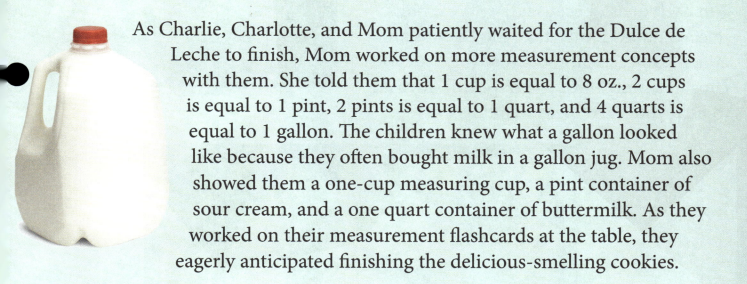

As Charlie, Charlotte, and Mom patiently waited for the Dulce de Leche to finish, Mom worked on more measurement concepts with them. She told them that 1 cup is equal to 8 oz., 2 cups is equal to 1 pint, 2 pints is equal to 1 quart, and 4 quarts is equal to 1 gallon. The children knew what a gallon looked like because they often bought milk in a gallon jug. Mom also showed them a one-cup measuring cup, a pint container of sour cream, and a one quart container of buttermilk. As they worked on their measurement flashcards at the table, they eagerly anticipated finishing the delicious-smelling cookies.

Teacher

You will need to gather measuring devices for 1 cup, 1 pint, 1 quart, and 1 gallon for Exercise 2. Also, gather items for a recipe you would enjoy making with students for Exercise 3.

Mr. M!

Today you will be putting together a "Mr. Measure" to help you better understand some of the measurements we have been learning about. To construct your "Mr. M," first cut out the figures on the next few pages, and sort them into piles. Next, take your gallon-sized "Mr. M" and attach the 4 quarts (his arms and legs) to him with brads, since we know that there are 4 quarts in a gallon. Now, take the 8 pints and attach 2 to each quart, because there are 2 pints in each quart. Lastly, take the 16 cups and attach 2 to each pint, because there are 2 cups in a pint. Now, you have "Mr. Measure" to help you learn measurements.

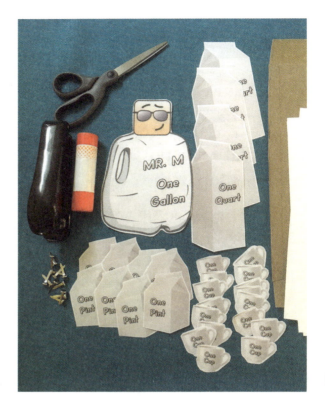

Name_____

 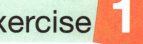

One
Pint

One
Pint

One
Pint

One
Pint

One
Pint

One
Pint

One
Pint

One
Pint

One
Pint

Fun with Measurements!

Today you will further explore the measurements of one cup (c.), one pint (pt.), one quart (qt.), and one gallon (gal.) by doing some hands-on experimenting. Take the measuring devices that you and your teacher have gathered and, using rice, begin measuring with the measuring cup (1 c.) and fill the pint container.

☐   How many cups are in the pint? _____ c.

☐   Now, take your one-cup measuring cup, and see how many cups are in a quart. Write your findings on the line here. _____ c.

☐   Next, take your one-cup measuring cup, and find out how many cups are in a gallon. Write the amount here. _____ c.

☐   How many pints are in a quart? _____ pt.

☐   How many pints are in a gallon? _____ pt.

☐   How many quarts are in a gallon? _____ qt.

☐   If your teacher allows you to, continue experimenting with these measurements using water (in the bathtub or sink).

Measurement Flashcards.

Today you will begin working on your measurement flashcards for cups, pints, quarts, and gallons.

Also, you will be following a recipe and cooking something with your teacher's help. You may follow one of the recipes from Hairo and Natalia in this lesson, or you may choose something out of a cookbook. In the box below, draw a picture of whatever you chose to make.

My Picture

Matching.
Match the correct picture with the clue provided. There may be more than one clue for each picture.

1.   There are 4 of me in a gallon.

2.   There are 2 of me in a quart.

3.   There are 4 of me in a quart.

4.   There are 16 of me in a gallon.

5.   There are 8 of me in a gallon.

6.   One of me holds 4 quarts.

7.   One of me holds 4 cups.

8.   One of me holds 2 cups.

9.   One of me holds 16 cups.

10. One of me holds 8 pints.

☐   Take out all the flashcards you have made this year. What a stack! Take the time to review all the flashcards you have made. You sure have learned a lot!

Copywork Time!

The twins really enjoyed making the recipes that their Peruvian friends sent! They want to write a thank you letter and send them one of their own favorite recipes. (In the space below write down one of your favorite recipes.)

My Favorite Recipe

Review Time!

Dear Hairo and Natalia,

Thank you so much for sending the recipes! We made them with Mom, and they were so yummy! We have been learning about measurements. Some units of measure are used to measure length, some are used to measure weight, while others are used to measure liquids. We have shown you how to measure temperature and length. This is how you measure liquid:

(Match the picture to the correct word)

1 gallon

1 quart

1 pint

1 cup

We also learned...

1 gallon = _____ quarts   1 quart = _____ pints   1 pint = _____ cups

Love,

Charlie, Charlotte, and our friend, _____

Count how many of each kind of animal or bird, and put the number in the circles below.

Review of Measurements

The recipes Hairo and Natalia had included in their letters to Charlie and Charlotte were definitely a hit! The family unanimously agreed that, although the cookies took awhile to make, they were delicious and well worth the wait. Also, the Potatoes with Cheese were very yummy!

It was now March, and the days were warming up, even into the 40s sometimes, and the days were definitely getting longer, with more light from the sun. Nights were still quite chilly, but this variance in temperature, with warmer days and cooler nights, meant that the sap was running in the maple trees. This, Dad explained, meant that they could tap the trees, which involved inserting a metal tube, called a spile, into the tree trunk. Next, Dad instructed the twins to hang a bucket on the metal tube in order to collect the flowing sap. Dad further explained that sap was actually made up of mostly water, so it would take as many as 40 gallons of sap to make even one gallon of maple syrup. To make the syrup from sap, they would need to boil the maple syrup until it reached a temperature 7°F above the boiling point of water, which the twins remembered was 212°F.

Charlie and Charlotte found this maple sap to syrup "sugaring process" quite fascinating and were quick to check the small buckets on the trees every day and empty them into the big containers of sap in the shed. They were so excited to collect enough sap to begin the boiling process, and they could hardly wait for Mom's Swedish pancakes smothered with the syrup they were helping Dad make.

Teacher

Exercise 5 of this Lesson is a Show and Tell Day. Please have these items available for your student: old magazines or fliers with pictures of food, craft items, and a large piece of poster board.

Review Time!

Work through these problems and write the answers. Use the space at the bottom of the page to work out the problems if you need to.

☐   How many inches in 1 foot? _____ inches

☐   How many inches in 2 feet? _____ inches

☐   How many inches in 3 feet? _____ inches

☐   How many inches in 4 feet? _____ inches

☐   How many inches in 5 feet? _____ inches

☐   How tall are you in feet and inches? (Have your teacher measure you)
        _____ feet _____ inches

☐   How tall is your teacher? _____ feet _____ inches

☐   How long is your bed? _____ feet _____ inches

☐   How long is your foot? _____ inches

☐   How long is your arm? _____ inches

☐   Review your measurement flashcards!

Review Time!

Word problems! Remember the steps.

1. There is a triangle with sides that measure 10 inches, 12 inches, and 3 inches. What is the perimeter of the triangle?

2. The twins measured the perimeter of Ella's playpen. They found that it was a rectangle which had two sides that were 4 feet long and two sides that were 3 feet long. What was the perimeter of Ella's playpen?

3. Charlotte is helping Mom with Ella's baby scrapbook. The scrapbook papers are square-shaped with 12-inch sides. What is the perimeter of one piece of paper?

4. Charlotte and Charlie have new jump ropes which are 5 feet long. How many inches are the ropes?

5. Mom is making a special supper for Dad's birthday, and the twins are decorating the dining room for a surprise party. It is 2:00 in the afternoon, and Dad is coming home at 5:30. How long do the twins have to decorate?

Review Time!

More word problems to solve!

1. When the twins were outside this morning, the thermometer read 40°F. Now it is 53°F. What is the difference in the temperature from morning until now?

2. Mom bought a 2-pound block of cheese. How many ounces is the block of cheese?

3. Last week the average temperature was 35°F, and this week, the average temperature has been 42°F. What is the difference in the average temperatures?

4. If it takes 40 gallons of sap to make 1 gallon of maple syrup, how many gallons of sap does it take to make 2 gallons of syrup?

5. **Big BONUS!** If there are 2 cups in 1 pint, how many cups are in 3 pints?

Review Time!
For copywork:

12 inches = 1 foot

16 ounces = 1 pound

4 quarts = 1 gallon

2 pints = 1 quart

2 cups = 1 pint

Sunday   Monday

Tuesday   Wednesday

Thursday   Friday

Saturday

Trace the outlined words below of the months.

January February

March April

May June

July August

September October

November December

Review Time!

Today is Show and Tell Day! Using the magazines or newspaper pages your teacher gives you, make a large (poster board size) poster showing through images what you have learned about measurement.

You can also choose to draw and color your poster. Have fun!

Help the driver bring the package to place in the truck.

Start

Adding Money — No Regrouping

Baking bread with Mom was a favorite pastime for Charlotte. Just last week, Mom had been asked by a woman in their church to bake several loaves of bread for the upcoming bake sale. All of the money raised from the bake sale would be sent to the orphanage in South America. The twins' parents and several other people from their church had gone there to assist with cleanup and rebuilding after a devastating flood last summer. Charlotte was thrilled to be a part of the baking project, which would be helping all of those young children at the orphanage, including her dear friend and pen pal, Natalia. All day, Charlotte and her mother mixed ingredients, kneaded dough, let the dough rise, punched the dough, formed loaves, and let the loaves rise. In the end, it was definitely worth it, as Charlotte and Mom watched beautiful loaves of delicious-smelling bread come out of the oven!

Each small loaf of bread at the bake sale was to sell for $ 1.30. If one loaf costs this much, how much will it cost for two loaves using vertical math?

$$\begin{array}{r} \$1.30 \\ +\ \$1.30 \\ \hline \$2.60 \end{array}$$

To solve any money problem, whether addition or subtraction, we need to, first of all, bring the decimal point straight down. Next, we begin at the far right column and add those two numbers, which, in this problem, are 0 + 0, which equals 0. Now, we move to the column just to the left of that column and add those two numbers, which, in this problem, are 3 + 3, which equals 6. We now move to next column to the left and add those numbers, which are 1 + 1, which equals 2. Lastly, we bring the dollar sign down since this a money problem. If we read this problem as written, it would read as follows: One dollar and ("and" is the word we use when we see a decimal point) thirty cents plus one dollar and thirty cents equals two dollars and sixty cents.

Here are some more problems to practice with using vertical math:

$$\begin{array}{r} \$2.52 \\ +\ \$1.15 \\ \hline \end{array}$$
$$\begin{array}{r} \$4.62 \\ +\ \$3.17 \\ \hline \end{array}$$

$$\begin{array}{r} \$3.13 \\ +\ \$4.84 \\ \hline \end{array}$$
$$\begin{array}{r} \$9.05 \\ +\ \$\ .13 \\ \hline \end{array}$$

Read the problems and their answers to your teacher.

Word Problem! Remember the steps.

A lady at the bake sale bought 2 delicious pies. One was a scrumptious triple berry pie which cost $4.15. The other pie was a beautiful apple pie which cost $3.50. How much did the lady pay all together?

Draw a pie in the space below. Cut the pie in half. Remember, true fractions have equal parts.

My Drawing

Addition.

$$\begin{array}{r} \$14.21 \\ +\ \$\ 3.47 \\ \hline \end{array}$$
$$\begin{array}{r} \$2.91 \\ +\ \$\ \ .07 \\ \hline \end{array}$$

$$\begin{array}{r} \$10.12 \\ +\ \$\ 3.25 \\ \hline \end{array}$$
$$\begin{array}{r} \$71.18 \\ +\$\ 2.16 \\ \hline \end{array}$$

Practice your doubles fact families with your flashcards.

Word Problems. Remember the steps.

1. Charlie had $4.55. Charlotte had $5.13. How much money did they have all together?

2. It cost $12.05 to send a package to Hairo and Natalia. Mom also bought stamps for $7.14. How much did she spend in all?

3. Charlie's favorite ice cream treat cost $1.75. Charlotte preferred a treat that cost $1.20. How much did the treats cost together?

4. Dad bought a new hammer at the hardware store. It cost $15.25. While he was there, he decided to buy a box of nails that were on sale for $4.10. How much did Dad spend at the hardware store?

5. Mom bought a bag of chickadee food for $5.69. She also picked up a bag of dried corn for the squirrels for $3.10. How much did she spend in all?

Color in the thermometers to show the correct temperatures.

34 °F   80 °F   95 °F   7 °F

Name_____

Additional Practice.

$$\begin{array}{r} \$21.41 \\ + \$15.01 \\ \hline \end{array} \qquad \begin{array}{r} \$15.01 \\ + \$\ 2.98 \\ \hline \end{array}$$

Count the following amounts using your counting money:

☐ 6 dimes

How much? _____¢ or $._____

☐   2 nickels and 6 pennies

How much? _____¢ or $._____

☐ 1 dime, 1 nickel, and 3 pennies

How much? _____¢ or $._____

☐ 1 quarter, 1 nickel, and 2 pennies

How much? _____¢ or $._____

Draw hands on the clocks to match the time below each.

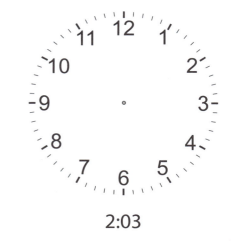

7:12   6:35   2:03

Review Time!

Write the place value of the underlined digit in each number.

<u>4</u>59 _____

2,2<u>3</u>9 _____

1<u>7</u> _____

<u>2</u>28 _____

<u>3</u>,672 _____

65<u>9</u> _____

Answer these questions by looking at the bar graph on the next page.

☐ How many chocolate cakes were sold? _____

☐ How many loaves of banana bread were sold? _____

☐ How many more apple pies sold than cherry pies? _____

☐ How many pies in all sold at the bake sale? _____

☐ How many more chocolate cakes sold than loaves of banana bread? _____

☐ How many cheesecakes and tea rings sold in all? _____

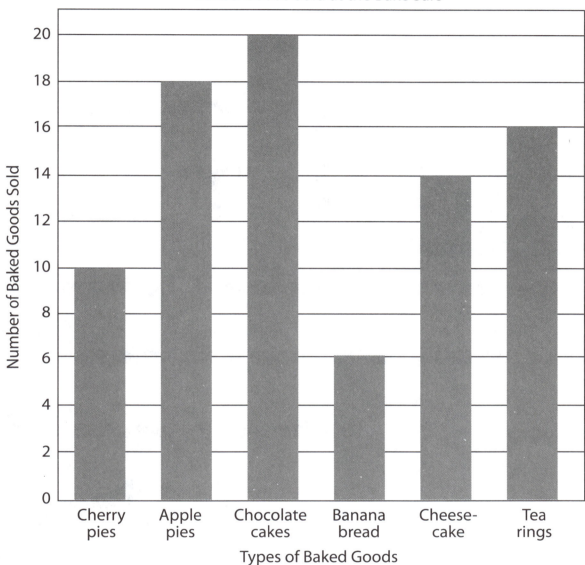

Baked Goods Sold at the Bake Sale

Help the man find the money he needs.

Finish

Start

Subtracting Money — Making Change

Playing with a ball in the house was against the rules, and now, the twins understood why. They had been having so much fun, but that changed the instant Mom's favorite lamp crashed to the floor and shattered into several pieces. Charlie and Charlotte knew they needed to go to Mom and explain what happened right away. Finding her in the living room rocking Ella, the twins found it incredibly hard to look her in the eye. Nevertheless, they forced themselves to.

"Mom, we have something to tell you," Charlie shifted uncomfortably and yet maintained eye contact with his mother.

"What is it?" Mom questioned with a very concerned look on her face.

Charlotte interjected now, "Well, we were playing with our new ball in the schoolroom, and we accidentally broke your favorite lamp. We are so sorry, Mom. Please forgive us." Charlotte began crying.

"Yeah, Mom, please forgive us," Charlie added, his voice cracking as tears made their way down his cheeks, too.

Tears coming to her eyes, Mom waited a few moments before responding. To Charlie and Charlotte, it seemed like an eternity! "Well, children, I am very sad. That lamp was a gift from your father and is special to me. I am, however, very thankful that you came to me right away and let me know. I do forgive you both," finished Mom.

The children, knowing that it was their disobedience which caused the lamp to break, now asked Mom to help them pray and ask God's forgiveness, too.

"Certainly. Let's pray together, Charlie and Charlotte." Mom laid Ella in her playpen and knelt with the twins to pray.

A few minutes later, after prayers were said and the three remained sitting by each other, Charlie said, "I am so thankful that God forgives us and that you forgive us too, Mom. But I do think Charlotte and I need to buy you another lamp for the schoolroom."

"I agree with Charlie," Charlotte chimed in.

"Okay, children," replied Mom, "next time we are in town, we will go look for a lamp and see what we can find."

The twins broke Mom's favorite lamp and wished to buy her another one. Charlie and Charlotte together had $8.50. They were fortunate enough to find Mom an almost-identical lamp at the consignment shop downtown. It only cost $5.00! How much did the twins have left after purchasing the lamp for their mother?

To solve this problem, we first need to notice it is a subtraction problem. Anytime we see the clue words "how much do they have left?" it tells us that we will be subtracting. Next, we need to line the decimal points up, just like in an addition money problem. We know the twins had $8.50, and $8.50 is larger than $5.00, so $8.50 is the top number, or minuend, of the subtraction problem. We know the lamp cost $5.00, and that number is smaller than $8.50, so $5.00, or the subtrahend, goes underneath the minuend. Now, we are ready to subtract!

$$\begin{array}{r} \$8.50 \\ -\$5.00 \\ \hline \$3.50 \end{array}$$

The first thing we need to do is move our decimal point straight down. Just like an addition problem involving money, we begin subtracting with the column on the far right, and then we go to the next column to the left of that column. Next, we go to the column to the left of the decimal point and subtract. Lastly, we move the dollar sign down. The answer in a subtraction problem is called the difference. Our problem now reads as follows: Eight dollars and fifty cents minus five dollars equals three dollars and fifty cents.

$$\begin{array}{r} \$9.99 \\ -\ \$8.52 \\ \hline \end{array} \qquad \begin{array}{r} \$8.52 \\ -\ \$6.11 \\ \hline \end{array} \qquad \begin{array}{r} \$7.32 \\ -\ \$1.20 \\ \hline \end{array} \qquad \begin{array}{r} \$9.57 \\ -\$\ .45 \\ \hline \end{array}$$

Word Problem!

Mom gave Charlie $5.25 to buy eggs when they stopped at the store. The eggs cost $1.10. How much was left to give back to Mom?

Divide the square into 4 equal parts. Label each part with the correct fraction.

Subtraction Review!

$$\begin{array}{r} \$4.12 \\ -\ \$2.02 \\ \hline \end{array} \qquad \begin{array}{r} \$9.82 \\ -\ \$5.61 \\ \hline \end{array}$$

$$\begin{array}{r} \$3.77 \\ -\ \$\ .20 \\ \hline \end{array} \qquad \begin{array}{r} \$6.49 \\ -\ \$2.48 \\ \hline \end{array}$$

Solve the following story problems. Remember the steps.

1. At the grocery store, Mom spent $21.42. She gave the cashier $22.42. How much change did Mom receive back?

2. The twins had been counting the number of birds at the feeders these days. This week they had counted 67 birds, but last week they had seen 89 birds. How many more birds did they see last week than this week?

3. Grandpa and Grandma had 55 new baby chicks at their farm. Last year at this time, they had 42. How many more baby chicks were born this year than last year?

4. Gas prices really had gone up in the past month. Last month, gas was $3.25 per gallon, and this month, gas was up to $3.79 per gallon. How much more did gas cost per gallon this month?

5. Ella took a two and a half hour nap yesterday. She went down for her nap at 2:30 in the afternoon. What time did she wake up?

Count the money and write the amount in the space provided.

_____ ¢

_____ ¢

_____ ¢

Practice.

$$\begin{array}{r} \$2.19 \\ -\ \$1.08 \\ \hline \end{array} \qquad \begin{array}{r} \$7.63 \\ -\ \$5.61 \\ \hline \end{array}$$

Count the following amounts using your counting money:

5 nickels   How much? _____¢ or $._____

1 nickel and 9 pennies   How much? _____¢ or $._____

3 dimes, 2 nickels, and 7 pennies   How much? _____¢ or $._____

2 quarters, 2 nickels, and 5 pennies How much? _____¢ or $._____

Draw hands on the clocks to match the time below each.

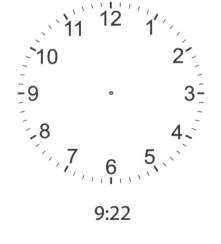 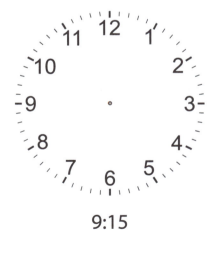 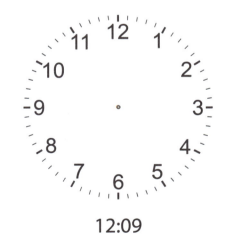

9:22   9:15   12:09

 =

Sometimes when we buy something, we do not have the exact amount of money to pay for the item. When this happens, we will receive change. For example, if we wanted to buy a bottle of juice that cost 60¢, and we only had a 1 dollar bill, what would we do? Look at the dollar and the dimes. We can see that 1 dollar equals 10 dimes. To see how much we would receive in change, cross out 60¢ in dimes. What is left? _____ ¢

To practice this concept, play store with your teacher. Gather some items from around the room and "price" them. This can be done by simply taping paper squares with prices onto the items. For example, you could "sell" your teacher the salt and pepper shakers for 50¢ or the napkin basket for 25¢. Keep all of your prices under 1 dollar and in increments of 5 or 10 (for example: 5¢, 10¢, 15¢, 20¢). Practice making change for your "customer" teacher.

More Work with Word Problems

Taking a week off for spring break, Charlie and Charlotte, Ella, and their parents set off for the perfect vacation. They were returning to Grandpa and Grandma's farm, where Charlie and Charlotte had been fortunate enough to spend the entire summer last year. They could hardly wait; the excitement was overwhelming them as they asked Dad, for the tenth time or so, how much longer it would be. Dad patiently responded that they would get there when they get there, and then he pulled into a gas station to fill up. Charlie, looking for a reason to get out and stretch his growing legs, jumped out of his seat and asked, "Could I please help you pump the gas, Dad?"

"You may get out and stretch and help me by washing the windshield," responded Dad, with a knowing chuckle.

As Charlie cleaned the windshield, his eyes were really fixed on watching the gas pump; he loved to see the numbers changing so rapidly.

"Wow, Dad!" Charlie exclaimed. "Fifty dollars — whoa! That is a lot!"

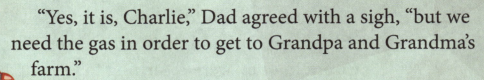

"Yes, it is, Charlie," Dad agreed with a sigh, "but we need the gas in order to get to Grandpa and Grandma's farm."

Stepping inside the station with Dad, Charlie was amazed at all there was to look at. This was not just a gas station; it was a bakery, a sporting goods store stocked with fishing rods and bait, a restaurant, and a convenience store! Dad smiled at Charlie and asked if he thought fresh cookies from the bakery would be a nice treat for each of them on their trip. Charlie excitedly nodded his head and went up to the cashier with Dad to pay for the cookies.

"Three dollars and sixty cents for the cookies and fifty dollars for the gas comes to fifty three dollars and sixty cents," announced the cashier.

$$\begin{array}{r} \$50.00 \\ +\ \$\ \ 3.60 \\ \hline \$53.60 \end{array}$$

Charlie had already figured that out in his head and coaxed Dad and Mom into quizzing Charlotte and him on their addition and subtraction facts to help pass time in the car. They also played a game where they looked for different states on license plates, they listened to a compelling story on the CD player, and they played an alphabet game, in which they tried to spy something for every letter of the alphabet. Time passed quickly, and very soon they arrived at the farm!

Copywork:

Steps to solve a word problem:

1. Read the problem.

2. What is the question?

3. Circle the numbers.

4. Think it through.

5. Check your answer.

These are some key words or clue words that will tell you what you need to do.

Addition Clue Words

How many all together?

How many in all?

Together?

Subtraction Clue Words

How many more?

What is left?

What is the difference?

How much longer (or shorter)?

What is the change (money)?

How much warmer (or colder)?

How much heavier?

Word Problems.

1. Charlie read 16 pages in his book last night. This afternoon, he read 16 more pages. How many pages did he read in all?

2. Grandma bought a puzzle for Charlotte that cost $2.10. She bought Charlie a model car which cost $2.35. How much did she spend in all?

3. The twins' Sunday school class saved $50.00 for a mission's project. The older children's class saved $36.50. How much did the two classes save in all?

4. At the pet store, the twins found a new food dish for Pokey. It cost $3.80. They also found a salt lick for their sheep that cost $5.18. How much did they spend at the pet store?

5. Charlie ate 6 pancakes before he proclaimed he was full. Charlotte could only eat 5. How many pancakes did they eat all together?

☐ Review your addition flashcards.

☐ Narrate to your teacher the clue words for addition word problems.

Solve the Word Problems.

1. Charlotte bought Ella a rattle which cost 60¢ at the consignment shop. She paid the cashier with a 1 dollar bill. What did she receive back in change?

2. Mom found 97¢ in change in her purse. She put 40¢ in Ella's piggy bank. How much did she have left?

3. The twins saw 12 cardinals at the feeder on Monday and 18 on Tuesday. How many more did they see on Tuesday than Monday?

4. Last fall, Charlotte was 48 inches tall. When Dad measured her yesterday, she was 52 inches tall. How much taller is Charlotte now than she was last fall?

5. Charlie weighed 49 pounds last fall. He now weighs 61 pounds. How many pounds did Charlie gain over the winter?

☐ Review your subtraction flashcards.

☐ Narrate to your teacher the clue words for subtraction word problems.

More Word Problems.

1. A gallon of milk costs $3.41. Dad picked up 2 gallons of milk on his way home from work. How much did he spend in all on the milk?

2. A book of postage stamps contains 20 stamps. If the twins need 6 of them for their letters, how many stamps will be left?

3. Charlie collects baseball cards. He has 10 cards, and Grandpa sent him 8 more. How many cards does he have in all?

4. Dad paid Charlie to help with the spring cleanup of the yard. He gave him 1 quarter, 4 dimes, and 2 nickels. How much did he pay him to help?

☐ Count nickels up to 1 dollar. How many? _____

☐ Set aside 8 of those nickels. How many are left? _____

☐ Count dimes up to 1 dollar. How many? _____

☐ Set aside 3 of those dimes. How many are left? _____

Review Time!

Help the children write a letter to Hairo and Natalia showing what they have been learning.

Dear Natalia and Hairo,

How are things in Peru? We are doing well. We have been keeping really busy. Dad taught us how to tap maple trees for collecting sap. We have been boiling the sap, and it has made the best-tasting maple syrup ever! It is a long process, though; it takes 40 gallons of sap to make 1 gallon of syrup.

Word problems are a lot of fun! These are the steps to do them:

1._____

_____

2._____

_____

3._____

_____

4._____

_____

5._____

_____

Love your friends,

Charlotte, Charlie, and our friend, _____

More Work with Telling Time

The week at Grandpa and Grandma's was flying by! Charlie and Charlotte enthusiastically pitched in with the chores. They fed the chickens, collected the eggs, collected full sap buckets from the maple trees and took them into Grandpa's shed to dump them into larger containers, and assisted Grandma with cooking and cleaning up the kitchen. They also helped milk the cows, slop the pigs, and play with the goats.

Hours were spent exploring around Grandpa and Grandma's property as well. The twins took their tree guide and bird guide into the woods and pretended to be explorers just discovering this new area. Charlie had a compass along, too, just in case they got lost. Grandpa had shown him how to use it a couple of days ago. Grandpa also had let them borrow his binoculars. So far they had seen a couple of bluebirds, some tree swallows, and some black-capped chickadees. Charlotte noticed a few dandelions by one of the outbuildings on the farm and several bright green blades of grass peeking up from the ground. Listening, the twins heard the robins singing and even spotted one building a nest. Some trees were beginning to bloom; the pair could see tiny leaves on the crabapple trees.

Intently listening and observing these signs of spring, the twins' exploration on this day was interrupted by the "ding-ding-ding" of Grandma's triangle lunch bell.

Hearing this, Charlie and Charlotte realized they were extremely hungry, and they raced back to the farmhouse.

Washing their hands and joining the adults at the table, Charlie and Charlotte excitedly began describing the morning's discoveries.

After lunch, the twins joined Grandpa in the living room for a story. It was one of their favorite Bible stories about a little boy who only had two fish and five loaves of bread, but was willing to share it with Jesus. Jesus performed a miracle and fed 5,000 people and still had 12 baskets left over! Charlie and Charlotte loved this story, and both wished they would have been that young boy who was able to listen to Jesus' teaching that day, share his lunch with Him, and witness Jesus performing a miracle!

Finishing the story, Grandpa announced, "I could use some help on this sunny, spring afternoon, picking up sticks and cleaning up the yard, if anyone is interested." The twins both popped up off the couch and headed outside on this beautiful day, ready to help Grandpa.

Draw hands on the clocks to match the time.

12:30   4:41   7:08

Write the correct time under each clock.

_____   _____   _____

It's three forty-two in the afternoon.

Show the time on the clock.

Write the time using digits. _____

What time was it one hour ago? _____

☐   Use your time concepts flashcards to review.

Write the time and fill in the clocks for each activity during your day.

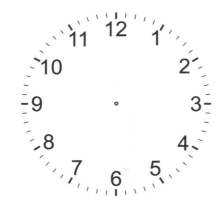

I get up in the morning at:

_____

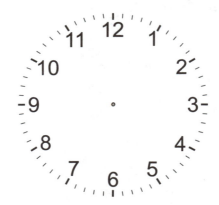

I take my bath at:

_____

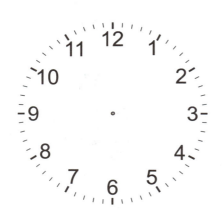

I eat breakfast at:

_____

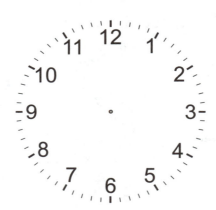

I go to bed at:

_____

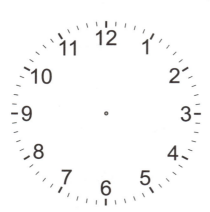

I do my chores at:

_____

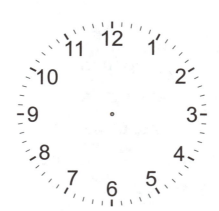

I go to church at:

_____

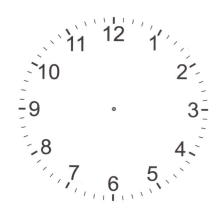

I start school time at:

_____

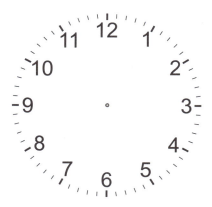

I have reading time at:

_____

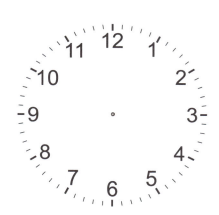

I have lunch at:

_____

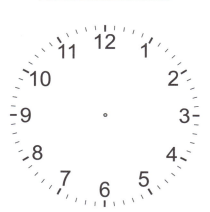

My snack time is at:

_____

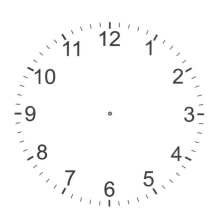

I have supper at:

_____

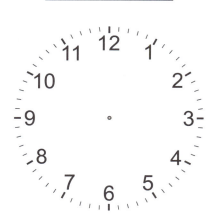

I play outside at at:

_____

It's eight fifteen in the morning.

Show the time on the clock.

Write the time using digits. _____

What time will it be in three hours?_____

It is three minutes after eleven o'clock in the morning.

Show the time on the clock.

Write the time using digits. _____

What time was it one hour ago? _____

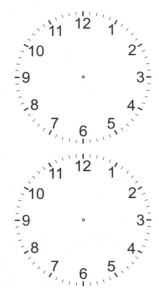

Tracing:

60 seconds = 1 minute

24 hours = 1 day

7 days = 1 week

12 months = 1 year

365 days = 1 year

52 weeks = 1 year

Note: Aadd the two new time concepts above to your flashcards!

In each of the boxes below, write the months of the year that go with that season.

Winter	Spring
1.	1.
2.	2.
3.	3.

Summer	Fall
1.	1.
2.	2.
3.	3.

Use your clock to show your teacher these times:

☐ 9:55   ☐ 1:01

☐ 2:07   ☐ 4:31

☐ 3:11   ☐ 6:43

☐ 5:09   ☐ 8:52

Review Time!

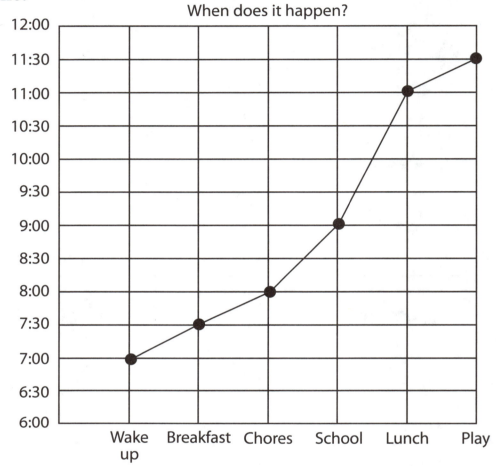

When does it happen?

Charlie's Morning Routine

Study the graph and answer these questions:

☐ What time does Charlie do his chores? _____

☐ What time does he play? _____

☐ What does he do first? _____

☐ What does he do at 9:00? _____

☐ How many hours from breakfast until lunch? _____

☐ What time is breakfast? _____

☐ **Optional**: On a separate sheet of paper, make a line graph charting your daily routine.

> *In the next lesson, we will be doing a project to provide students with real life application of the measurement concepts we have been studying and learning about this year. Please gather the following items:* — **Teacher**

1. 4 square pieces of material which measure 12 inches on all sides (4 different light colors would be best, or white/off white)
2. Fabric or permanent markers in bright colors
3. Your favorite color of yarn and a large needle with a large eye
4. Thread in whatever color you wish in a sewing needle
5. Material (whatever kind you wish) for backing (about 24 inches square)
6. **Optional:** Thin batting (about 24 inches square)
7. Fabric scissors
8. Measuring tape
9. Iron
10. Straight pins

Connect the Dots

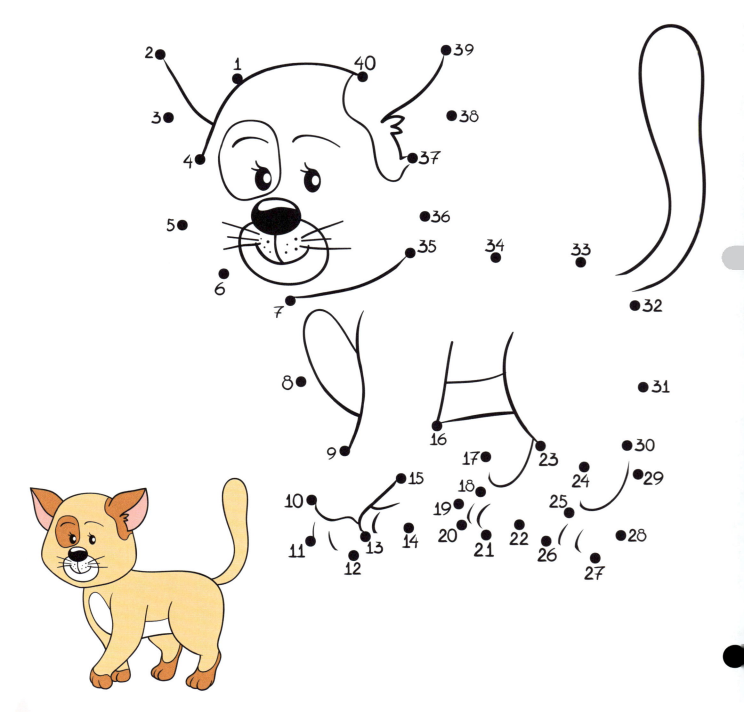

More Work with Measurements

Back at home now, after their wonderful vacation with Grandpa and Grandma, Charlie and Charlotte were outside playing with their sheep, Ann and Andy. Skipping happily along with the twins, the sheep seemed as thrilled as the children with this gorgeous weather! Pokey, whose "house" was outside today, was sunning himself on his rock; he seemed peaceful and happy, too.

Mom even brought Ella outside to enjoy the 70°F temperature and beautiful spring weather. Ella was growing quickly and already was five months old. She giggled at Charlie and Charlotte and could almost sit up by herself. At her last appointment, she was 33 inches tall and weighed in at 16 pounds, 1 ounce. Mom, Charlie, and Charlotte especially enjoyed taking Ella on their nature walks. She loved her stroller and seemed to observe everything as they hiked along.

With the beautiful weather, Dad's work was very busy, too. He was extremely grateful for his construction job and for days like these, when he could accomplish a lot at work.

Hairo and Natalia were doing well, too. In their last letter to the twins, they told of the things they were learning in the school at the orphanage, and they thanked Charlie and Charlotte for helping them and for being their friends and pen pals.

The family truly did have so much to be thankful for. Grandpa had reminded them at Thanksgiving that every day is a day to give thanks, and that is just what they decided to do. Thanking God for each other, for a beautiful spring day, for health and strength, for hard work, for friends and family near and far, and for shelter was the right thing to do. God was their Protector, their Provider, and they were incredibly blessed!

Measuring Project for the Lesson Making a Quilt

Materials needed:

1. 4 square pieces of material which measure 12 inches on all sides (4 different light colors would be best, or white/off white)

2. Fabric or permanent markers in bright colors

3. Your favorite color of yarn and a large needle with a large eye

4. Thread in whatever color you wish and a sewing needle

5. Material (whatever kind you wish) for backing (about 24 inches square)

6. **Optional**: thin batting (about 24 inches square)

7. Fabric scissors **(with teacher permission)**

8. Measuring tape (for sewing)

9. Iron **(with teacher permission)**

10. Straight pins

Directions: Before starting, make sure the fabric is washed, dried, and ironed. Please read all the directions before you start!

1. After your material is ironed, lay the four fabric squares so that they form one large square, arranged in the color scheme of your choice.

2. Take the two top squares, and lay them one on top of the other, right sides together.

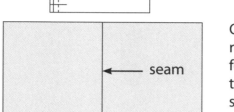

Have your teacher to pin together with straight pins. Using needle and thread, sew the pinned edge $\frac{1}{4}$ inch from the edge.

Open to show rectangle formed by the two squares sewn together.

seam

3. Do the same with the bottom two squares.

4. Lay the two rectangles on top of each other with right sides together. Pin $\frac{1}{4}$ inch from the edge and sew.

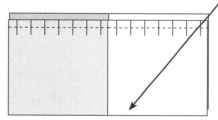

5. Open up the material to reveal your large square, with all inside seams sewn together.

6. Measure your square with your measuring tape, and then measure and cut a piece of backing (and thin batting, if desired) to fit the size of the square.

7. Lay the large square and the backing on top of each other, right sides together. Pin $\frac{1}{4}$ inch from the edge around three sides and sew. Leave the fourth side open. You will have created a large "pocket."

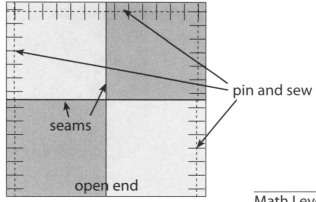

pin and sew

seams

open end

8. Turn your "pocket" right side out and iron to flatten seams. Insert batting. Turn $\frac{1}{4}$ inch of both front and back of open end toward the inside of "pocket" and iron. Pin and sew folded edges closed.

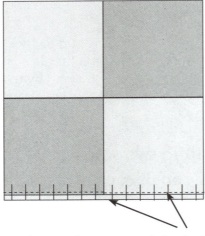

Fold and iron these edges toward the inside of the "pocket." Pin and sew to close opening.

9. Use your markers to draw or write in each square. Suggestion: Draw a picture from your favorite story book(s), or you could make a memory quilt by drawing a favorite memory.

10. Cut five 9-inch pieces of yarn. Using your large needle, start at the front of your quilt (right in the middle where the four pieces intersect), and go down through all the layers. Come back up right next to where you went through. Pull the ends of the yarn even and and tie it tightly. Do this with the other four pieces of yarn in the center of each square. Now show everyone your quilt!

☐ Calendar reminder! Make sure your calendar is up to date!

Review of Place Value Through the Thousands' Place

This week you will be reviewing place value through the 1,000s place. Remember that you have special counting manipulatives for counting much bigger numbers! Do one section each day.

First, let's work with the concept of how numbers move from 10s to 100.

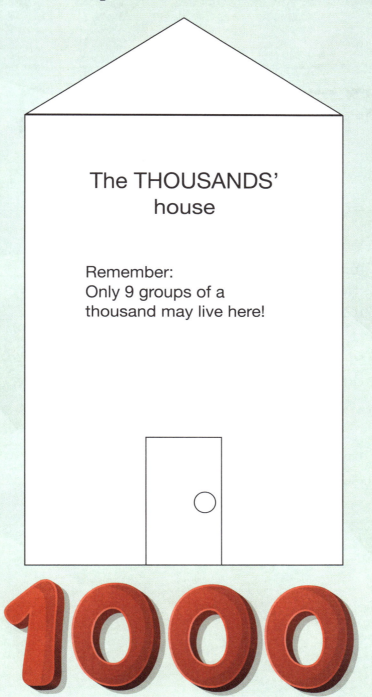

The THOUSANDS' house

Remember:
Only 9 groups of a
thousand may live here!

1000

Copy these numbers and say them out loud to your teacher. Narrate what you know about how these numbers go together.

90   91   92   93   94   95

96   97   98   99   100

When we have 99 items, we have _____ groups of 10 and _____ groups of one.

What is the next number? _____

How many groups of 10 can live in the Tens' house? When we have more than 9 groups of 10, what do we do? (Narrate orally to your teacher.)

Now let's work with the next group of numbers.

Copy these numbers and say them out loud to your teacher. Narrate what you know about how these numbers go together.

100 101 102 103 104 105

106 107 108 109 110

Use your counters to show your teacher these numbers. (Place a 100 counter in the Hundreds' House and the correct number of counters in the Tens' and Ones' Houses.) Narrate to your teacher what each 100 counter stands for.

When we have 109 items, we have _____ groups of 100, _____ groups of 10, and _____ groups of 1.

What is the next number? _____

Now let's look at what happens when we reach the end of the first group of 100. Copy these numbers and say them out loud to your teacher. Narrate what you know about how the numbers go together.

190 191 192 193 194 195

196   197   198   199   200

Use your counters to show your teacher these numbers. When we have 199 items, we have _____ groups of 100, _____ groups of 10, and _____ groups of 1. What is the next number? _____

With your counting items and 100s counters, show your teacher what happens when you count from 199 to the next number, 200. How many groups of 10 can stay in the Tens' house? _____ How many groups of 1 can stay in the Ones' house? _____

Work with these concepts until you are comfortable with them. It is important to completely understand place value concepts before moving on in mathematics.

Now let's look at what happens when we reach the end of another group of 100. Copy these numbers and say them out loud to your teacher. Narrate WHAT you know about how the numbers go together.

490 491 492 493 494 495

496 497 498 499 500

Use your counters to show your teacher these numbers. When we have 499 items, we have _____ groups of 100, _____ groups of 10, and _____ groups of 1.

What number comes next? _____

What do you do with your counters when you reach this number? Narrate to your teacher. Now copy these numbers.

790 791 792 793 794 795

796 797 798 799 800

Do you see the pattern? Explain it to your teacher. When we reach the end of a group of 700 items, and we want to move onto the 800s, what do we do?

Today, let's look at another group of numbers. Copy these numbers and say them out loud.

990 991 992 993 994 995

996   997   998   999   1,000

Look at the number 999. How many groups of a hundred does it have? _____

How many groups of ten? _____

How many groups of one? _____

Show your teacher the numbers above using your 100s counters and counting items.

Narrate to your teacher what you are doing as you count these numbers with your counters: 998, 999, 1,000.

Explain to your teacher what happened when you went from 999 to 1,000.

Review Time!

Use your counters and Place Value Village to show these numbers. Narrate what you are doing.

- ☐ 765
- ☐ 543
- ☐ 267
- ☐ 912
- ☐ 333
- ☐ 498
- ☐ 816
- ☐ 1,000
- ☐ 291

Are there any place value concepts that you are still not completely understanding? Talk to your teacher about it. Use your Place Value Village to show your teacher what you know about place value.

Teacher

Take this opportunity to assess how well your student understands place value. Of all math concepts, this one can be the trickiest! More than anything, it takes practice and discussion.

Connect the Dots

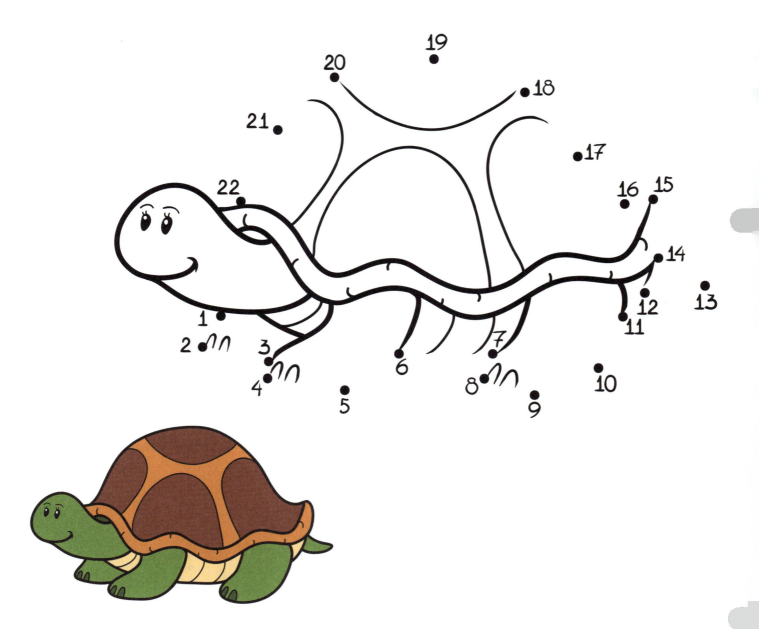

Review of Word Problems — the Steps of Solving

It's time to review the steps to solve a word problem:

1. Read the problem carefully.
2. Ask "what is the question?"
3. Circle the numbers you will need to use to solve the problem.
4. Think it through.
   Will you need to add or subtract? There are key or clue words that will tell you what you need to do. If your word problem has the words "all together," you know you will need to add, because adding will tell you what everything together is. If your word problem has the words "what is the difference," you know you will need to subtract. Subtracting will tell you how much more or less one number is than another.
5. The last step is to check your answers.

Remember your clue words:

Addition Clue Words	**Subtraction Clue Words**
How many all together?	How many more?
How many in all?	What is left?
Together?	What is the difference?
	How much longer (or shorter)?
	What is the change (money)?
	How much warmer (or colder)?
	How much heavier?

Work through one section each day.

Word Problems.

Circle numbers and underline key words.

1. The twins have enjoyed writing to their friends at the orphanage in South America. They have written 4 letters to their friends, and they plan to write 3 more before the spring is over. How many letters will they write all together?

2. Charlie has been practicing archery with the bow and arrow that Grandpa gave him. He hit the target 6 times yesterday and 8 times today. How many times did Charlie hit the target all together?

3. Charlotte and Mom made 24 cookies on Monday and 24 more cookies on Tuesday. How many cookies did they make all together?

4. When Dad built the fire in the fireplace on a cold spring night, he used 4 logs. The next night, he used 7 logs. How many logs did Dad use in the fireplace all together?

5. Charlie and Charlotte were excited to go shopping. They each had $25 dollars to spend! They bought 2 gifts for their grandparents, and 4 gifts for their parents and little sister. How many gifts did they buy all together?

Word Problems.

Circle numbers and underline key words.

1. Charlie used to have 7 pairs of pants that fit him. Since fall he has grown so much that only 4 pairs fit him now. How many pairs of pants does Charlie have left that fit?

2. Charlotte picked 10 beautiful leaves to use for her fall project. When she got them home, Mom told her that 2 of the leaves could not be used because they had caterpillar eggs on them. How many leaves does Charlotte have left to use for her project?

3. When Grandma came to visit the twins and their parents, she brought 6 pans of her yummy cinnamon rolls. She put 4 of the pans in the freezer for later. How many pans of rolls did Grandma have left for breakfast?

4. After Grandpa helped the twins with their new bird feeder, the children watched for new birds to come to their yard. On Monday they saw 10 chickadees, and on Tuesday they saw 7 cardinals. How many more chickadees than cardinals came to their feeder on Monday than Tuesday?

5. The children had so much fun helping plant flowers for spring! Charlie planted 3 yellow trillium, while Charlotte planted 5 daffodils. How many more flowers did Charlotte plant?

Word Problems.

Circle numbers and underline key words.

1. Charlie loves cookies! He ate 2 for a snack and wanted 4 more later in the afternoon. If Mom had said he could, how many cookies would Charlie have eaten?

2. The family took time to sing some hymns. They sang 5 slow hymns and 4 fast hymns. How many songs did they sing all together?

3. Grandma's new throw blanket was beautiful! Mom had made it from all sorts of soft fabric pieces. The throw was warm and cozy and perfect for snuggling under! The twins counted the squares that Mom had sewn together to make the front. Charlie counted 10 and Charlotte counted 8. How many squares were on the front of Grandma's new, cozy throw blanket?

4. Grandpa and Dad had put together a surprise for the twins. They took the children outside to see their new . . . bikes! After dinner, Dad took the twins out to ride them. Charlie took 15 trips up and down the hill on his bike, while Charlotte took 12 trips. How many trips did the twins make all together?

Perimeter Word Problems.

Circle numbers and underline key words.

1.　When Mom made pastries, she rolled out squares of dough that were 5 inches on all sides. What was the perimeter of each square of dough?

2.　The children measured the door to their playhouse. It was a rectangle that was 4 feet on two sides and 2 feet on the other two sides. What is the perimeter of their playhouse door?

3.　The twins were making paper airplanes with their grandma. For the first step, they folded their papers into triangles that were 10 inches on two sides and 7 inches on one side. What was the perimeter of the triangles?

4.　The twins were very excited! Dad promised to take them out in the mud as soon as the rain stopped. They always had fun making shapes in the mud with their boots. Charlie made a rectangle that was 10 feet long on two sides and 4 feet long on the other two sides. What was the perimeter of Charlie's track rectangle?

Review Time!

Discuss with your teacher the steps of solving a word problem. Dictate or write the steps below.

Time to review adding and subtracting when you have double digits in the problem.

Let's work again with our Place Value Village!

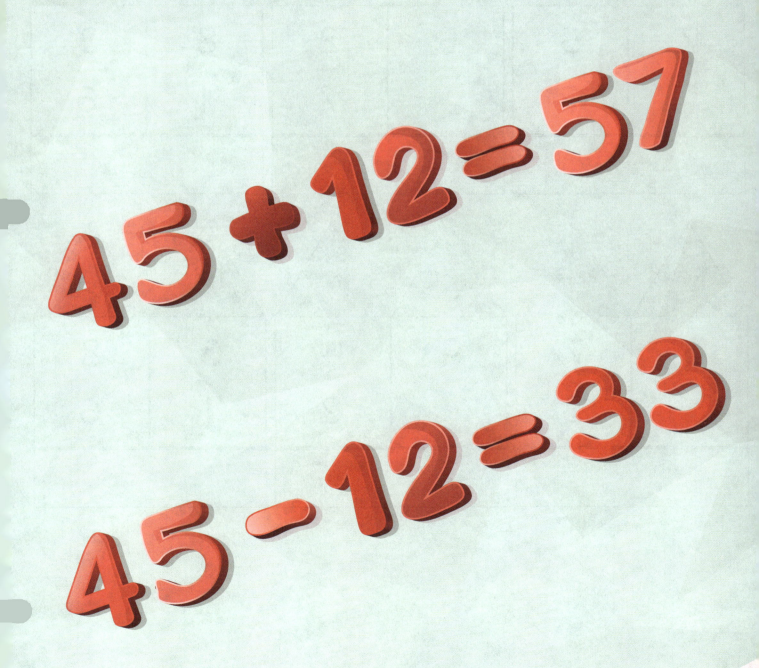

$$45 + 12 = 57$$

$$45 - 12 = 33$$

Review Time!

Narrate to your teacher the steps of solving each problem.

Tens	Ones
7	5
+	2

Tens	Ones
5	2
+	7

Tens	Ones
8	3
+ 1	6

Tens	Ones
5	7
−	3

Tens	Ones
9	4
−	2

Tens	Ones
3	8
− 1	6

Review Time!

Narrate to your teacher the steps of solving each problem.

Tens	Ones		Tens	Ones		Tens	Ones
5	4		7	1		3	8
+ 2	4		+ 2	7		+ 5	0

Tens	Ones		Tens	Ones		Tens	Ones
9	2		6	4		7	9
- 5	1		- 5	2		- 3	4

Review Time!

Narrate to your teacher the steps of solving each problem.

Tens	Ones
4	3
+ 2	8

Tens	Ones
8	6
+	4

Tens	Ones
1	5
+ 2	6

Tens	Ones
9	1
- 8	9

Tens	Ones
3	2
- 2	7

Tens	Ones
5	1
- 4	5

Review Time!

Narrate to your teacher the steps of solving each problem.

Tens	Ones
6	3
+ 2	7

Tens	Ones
7	4
+ 1	8

Tens	Ones
9	2
+	5

Tens	Ones
7	3
- 4	8

Tens	Ones
9	7
- 3	8

Tens	Ones
8	1
- 5	2

Review Time!

More word problems to review.

1. Charlie had 25 pinecones in his collection, and Charlotte had 17 rocks in hers. How many items did the twins have in their collections?

2. When Mom made cookies, she made 72 ginger cookies. She gave 36 to the elderly couple next door. How many did she have left?

3. The family drove 86 miles to a water park for a long weekend with Grandma and Grandpa. While they were there, they drove an additional 5 miles to a wonderful family restaurant. How many miles did they drive in all?

Reword Bonus!

Charlie had 16 toy cars. He lost 9 of them while playing in the sandbox in the fall.

Dad bought him a package of 6 toy cars for his birthday. Now how many does he have?

Review of Money Concepts

Remember when we were learning about money — the different kinds of coins and paper money? It's time to review what we learned!

Complete one section a day.

☐   Calendar reminder! Make sure your calendar is up to date.

Review Time!
Count out the following amounts for your teacher.

☐ $ .89

☐ $ .04

☐ $ .99

☐ $ .17

☐ $ 1.53

☐ $ 3.66

☐ $ 2.27

☐ $ 1.01

☐ $ 4.31

☐ $ 5.77

Your teacher just bought something at your "store." It cost $1.50, and they gave you $2.00. How much are you going to give back in change? Cross out the quarters that they spent. Circle what you will give them back in change.

 =

Review Time!

Read through each of the problems above. Remember the decimal point is another way of saying "and" when you have something in the "dollar" place. Narrate what you are doing as you work out the answer.

$$\begin{array}{r} \$\,1.23 \\ +\ \$\,2.76 \\ \hline \end{array} \qquad \begin{array}{r} \$\,5.64 \\ +\ \$\,1.20 \\ \hline \end{array}$$

$$\begin{array}{r} \$\,9.82 \\ +\ \$\ \ .15 \\ \hline \end{array} \qquad \begin{array}{r} \$\,6.92 \\ +\ \$\,1.07 \\ \hline \end{array}$$

Review Time!

$$\begin{array}{r} \$9.77 \\ -\ \$2.77 \\ \hline \end{array}$$

$$\begin{array}{r} \$5.69 \\ -\ \$1.43 \\ \hline \end{array}$$

$$\begin{array}{r} \$8.45 \\ -\ \$3.21 \\ \hline \end{array}$$

$$\begin{array}{r} \$6.36 \\ -\ \$5.16 \\ \hline \end{array}$$

Read through each of the problems above. Narrate what you are doing as you work out the answer.

Review Time! How much money is shown in the pictures below? Write your answer beside each picture.

   _____

 _____

 _____

_____

_____

Review Time!

Count the following amounts using your counting money:

7 nickels   How much? _____¢ or $._____

2 nickels and 11 pennies   How much? _____¢ or $._____

2 dimes, 1 nickel, and 9 pennies   How much? _____¢ or $._____

3 quarters, 1 nickel, and 11 pennies   How much? _____¢ or $._____

Play Store!

Gather some items and "price" them. This can be done by simply taping paper squares with prices onto the items. For example, you could "sell" your teacher the salt and pepper shakers for 50¢ or the napkin basket for 25¢. Keep all of your prices under 1 dollar and in increments of 5 or 10 (for example: 5¢, 10¢, 15¢, 20¢ . . .). Practice making change for your "customer" teacher.

Color by Number

Each number from 1 to 8 has been given a color. Find the numbers in the image and fill in each area with the correct color. For example, all the number 1s should be light blue. If you don't have the color assigned to a number, simply choose a similar color that you do have.

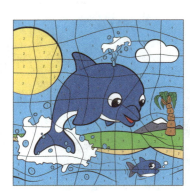

Review of Time and Temperature

It's time to review what we have learned about time and temperature.

Complete one section each day.

Review Time!

Draw hands on each clock to show the correct time.

12:09

11:23

6:55

What time is it? _____

What time will it be in two hours? _____

What time was it an hour ago? _____

Review Time! Color the thermometers to match the temperature.

28 °F   70 °F   54 °F   112 °F

What time is it?

_____   _____   _____

Review Time! Using your thermometer that you made in Lesson 21, show your teacher these temperatures.

☐	21°F	☐	72°F
☐	5°F	☐	0°F
☐	33°F	☐	109°F
☐	-10°F	☐	44°F

Using your clock that you made in Lesson 13, show your teacher these times.

☐   5:21

☐   3:46

☐   1:10

☐   2:09

☐   12:11

☐   10:45

☐   6:30

☐   8:27

☐   11:17

☐   2:05

☐   7:01

☐   9:52

☐   4:03

☐   3:48

Review Time!

What time is it? _____

What time will it be in four hours? _____

What time was it two hours ago? _____

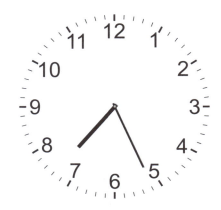

What time is it? _____

What time will it be in six hours? _____

What time was it five hours ago? _____

What time is it? _____

What time was it thirty minutes ago? _____

Review Time! What is the temperature?

_____ °F   _____ °F   _____ °F   _____ °F

Go through all of your temperature and time concepts flashcards. Narrate to your teacher what you have learned this year about both temperature and time.

Review of Addition and Subtraction Fact Families

Make fact families with the following groups of numbers. The first one is done for you.

4 6 10	2 8 10	3 9 12
4 + 6 = 10 6 + 4 = 10 10 − 6 = 4 10 − 4 = 6		

7 9 16	3 8 11	6 7 13

8   9   17

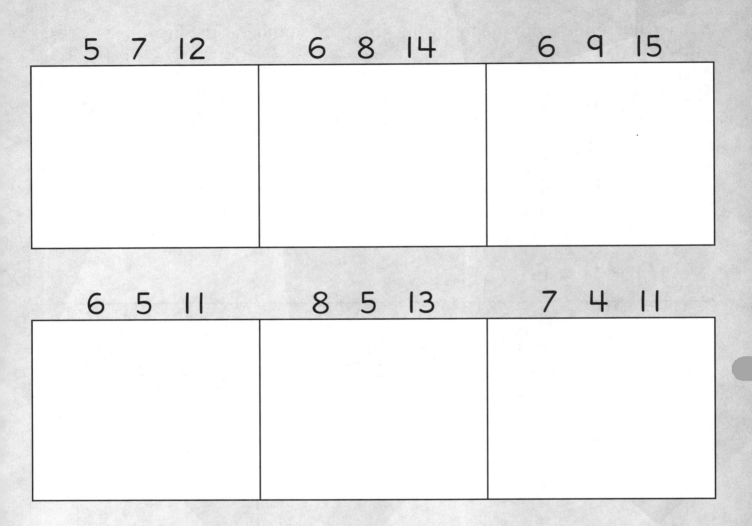

5 7 12	6 8 14	6 9 15

6 5 11	8 5 13	7 4 11

On the following page, you will be creating a page of math opposites. For example:

Adding is opposite of subtracting because the answer to an addition problem is bigger than both of the numbers added together. The answer to a subtraction problem is smaller than both of the other numbers in the problem.

Think of any other math opposites you have learned this year!

Math Opposites

Congratulations!
You Are Finished!

Manipulatives Section

- Place Value Village (pages 327–331)

- Place Value Village Counting Mat (page 333)

- Hundreds Counter (page 335)

- My 100s' Chart – blank on one side (pages 337–338)

- Number Cards (page 339)

- Larger Addition Mat / Larger Subtraction Mat (pages 341–343)

- Addition Fact Sheet (page 345)

- Subtraction Fact Sheet (page 346)

- My Addition Mat – horizontal side (page 347)

- My Addition Mat– vertical side (page 348)

- Doubles Families Fact Sheet (page 349)

- Right Brain Flashcards (page 351)

- Calendar – Master (page 352)

My 100s' Chart

0	1	2	3	4	5	6	7	8	9
10	11	12	13	14	15	16	17	18	19
20	21	22	23	24	25	26	27	28	29
30	31	32	33	34	35	36	37	38	39
40	41	42	43	44	45	46	47	48	49
50	51	52	53	54	55	56	57	58	59
60	61	62	63	64	65	66	67	68	69
70	71	72	73	74	75	76	77	78	79
80	81	82	83	84	85	86	87	88	89
90	91	92	93	94	95	96	97	98	99
100									

Directions: Remove from book and laminate. Blank chart on reverse side.

My 100s' Chart

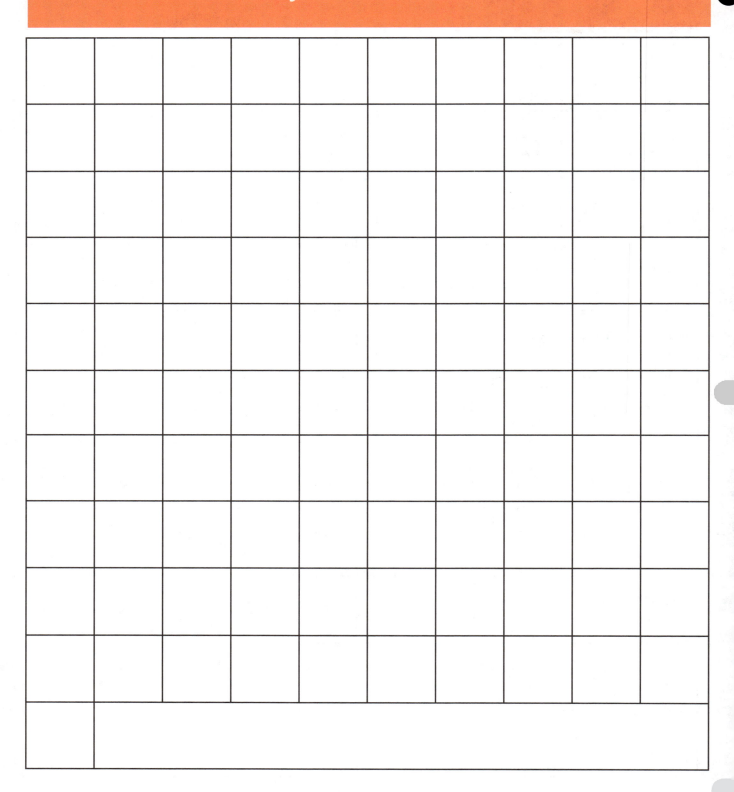

Directions: Blank chart for you to write on. Remove from book and laminate. Use washable markers.

0	1	2	3
4	5	6	7
8	9	10	11
12	13	14	15
16	17	18	19
20			

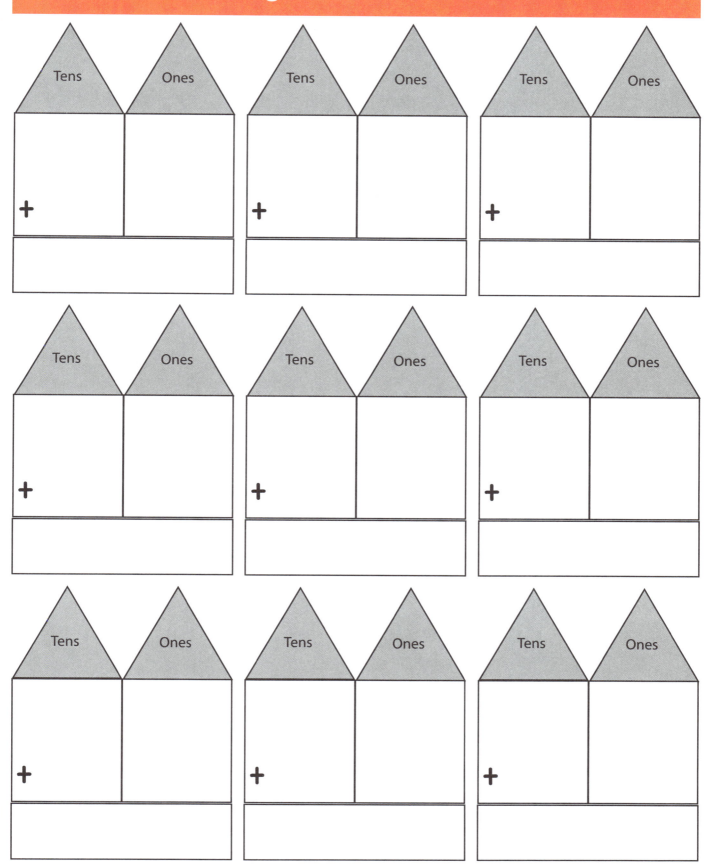

Directions: Remove from book and laminate. Use washable markers or dry erase. Blank chart on reverse side.

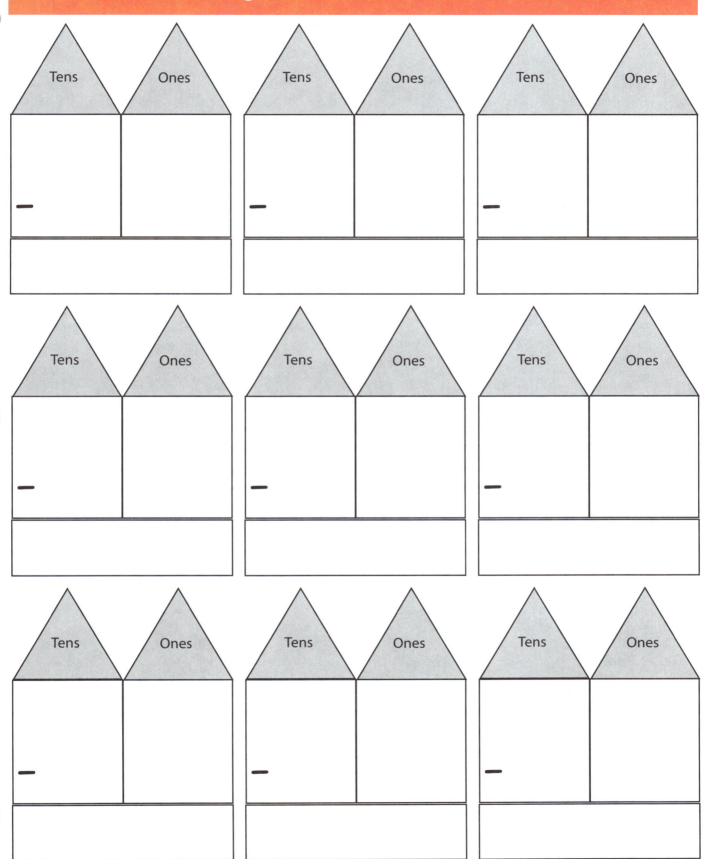

Directions: Remove from book and laminate. Use washable markers or dry erase. Blank chart on reverse side.

3 + 1 =	4 + 1 =	5 + 1 =	6 + 1 =
3 + 2 =	4 + 2 =	5 + 2 =	6 + 2 =
3 + 3 =	4 + 3 =	5 + 3 =	6 + 3 =
3 + 4 =	4 + 4 =	5 + 4 =	6 + 4 =
3 + 5 =	4 + 5 =	5 + 5 =	6 + 5 =
3 + 6 =	4 + 6 =	5 + 6 =	6 + 6 =
3 + 7 =	4 + 7 =	5 + 7 =	6 + 7 =
3 + 8 =	4 + 8 =	5 + 8 =	6 + 8 =
3 + 9 =	4 + 9 =	5 + 9 =	6 + 9 =
7 + 8 =	8 + 9 =	7 + 9 =	8 + 6 =

Directions: Carefully pull this page out of your book and laminate with contact paper. Use with washable or dry erase markers.

Subtraction Fact Sheet

7 - 3 =	10 - 2 =	13 - 7 =	12 - 8 =
8 - 3 =	15 - 6 =	10 - 4 =	19 - 9 =
9 - 5 =	17 - 8 =	13 - 6 =	13 - 9 =
9 - 4 =	11 - 7 =	15 - 7 =	13 - 4 =
11 - 4 =	15 - 8 =	14 - 9 =	12 - 5 =
11 - 8 =	14 - 6 =	16 - 7 =	16 - 9 =
11 - 2 =	13 - 8 =	14 - 8 =	12 - 6 =
11 - 9 =	15 - 9 =	14 - 5 =	18 - 9 =
11 - 6 =	17 - 9 =	12 - 7 =	16 - 8 =
11 - 3 =	10 - 6 =	12 - 4 =	14 - 7 =
11 - 5 =	13 - 5 =	10 - 8 =	20 - 10 =

Directions: Carefully pull this page out of your book and laminate with contact paper. Use with washable or dry erase markers.

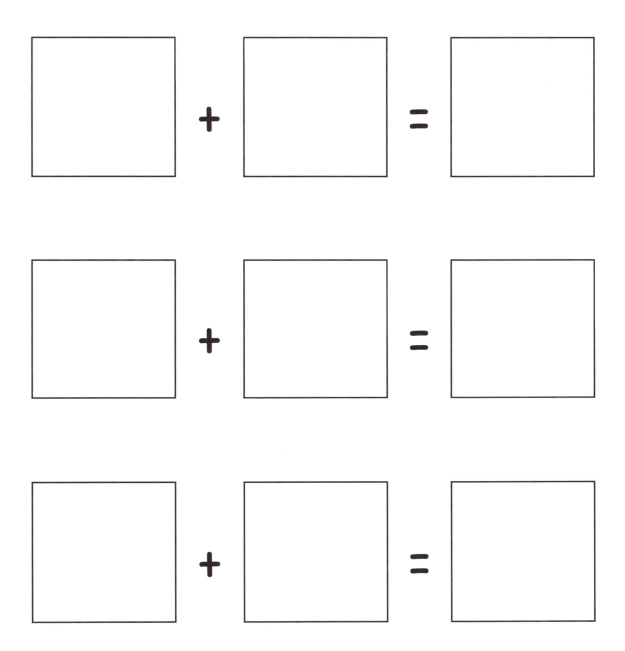

Directions: Carefully pull this page out of your book and laminate with contact paper. Use with washable or dry erase markers.

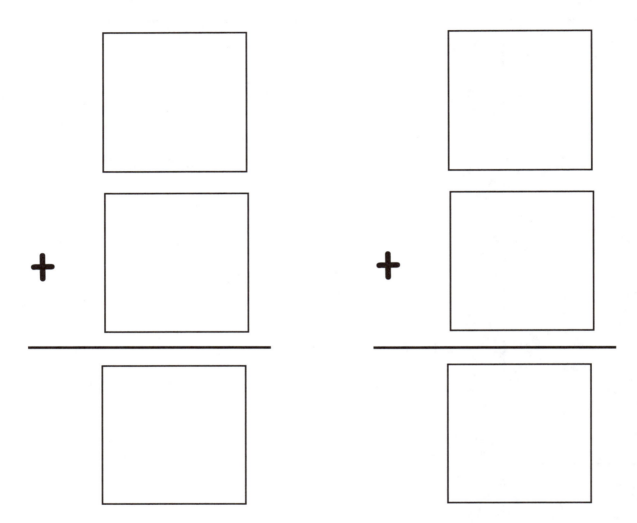

Directions: Carefully pull this page out of your book and laminate with contact paper. Use with washable or dry erase markers.

Doubles Families Fact Sheet

3 + 3 =	7 + 7 =	8 – 4 =	18 – 9 =
4 + 4 =	8 + 8 =	6 – 3 =	14 – 7 =
5 + 5 =	9 + 9 =	12 – 6 =	10 – 5 =
6 + 6 =	10 + 10 =	16 – 8 =	20 – 10 =

3 + 7 = 7 + 3 = 10 – 3 = 10 – 7 =	6 + 9 = 9 + 6 = 15 – 9 = 15 – 6 =	7 + 9 = 9 + 7 = 16 – 9 = 16 – 7 =
8 + 9 = 9 + 8 = 17 – 9 = 17 – 8 =	7 + 5 = 5 + 7 = 12 – 5 = 12 – 7 =	7 + 6 = 6 + 7 = 13 – 6 = 13 – 7 =
8 + 4 = 4 + 8 = 12 – 4 = 12 – 8 =	8 + 3 = 3 + 8 = 11 – 3 = 11 – 8 =	7 + 4 = 4 + 7 = 11 – 4 = 11 – 7 =
6 + 8 = 8 + 6 = 14 – 8 = 14 – 6 =	7 + 8 = 8 + 7 = 15 – 8 = 15 – 7 =	5 + 9 = 9 + 5 = 14 – 9 = 14 – 5 =

Directions: Carefully pull this page out of your book and laminate with contact paper. Use with washable or dry erase markers.

Right Brain Flashcards

What are "right brain" flashcards?

Right brain flashcards teach a concept by giving the "whole" story. Most flashcards are plain-colored and are missing the answer. Right brain flashcards teach a fact by giving the child a story to remember.

Use large index cards.

How to make right brain flashcards

1. Involve your student. Have them help you come up with a funny story that shows a math fact. (Look below for a sample flashcard.)

2. Have students help make their flashcards. We want students to OWN their own education. The sooner they take responsibility for their learning, the better.

3. Use color, texture, and words on your flashcards:

4. Make them double-sided. In this math program, students are going to be making their flashcards with vertical addition on one side and horizontal on the other. Use the same story on both sides.

5. Review often, and have students tell their math stories from their flashcards.

Punch a hole in the card and place it on a ring.

Month _____						
Sunday	Monday	Tuesday	Wednesday	Thursday	Friday	Saturday

Math Level 2 – Manipulatives